THE [IM]POSSIBLE DREAM

First published in the United Kingdom by the Evangelical Alliance in 2019

Evangelical Alliance
176 Copenhagen Street
London
N1 0ST

Printed and bound by Kingdom Print
ISBN 978-1-9163031-0-2

The Evangelical Alliance. A company limited by guarantee.
Registered in England & Wales No. 123448.
Registered Charity No England and Wales: 212325, Scotland: SC040576.

Contents

Steve Clifford

General director, Evangelical Alliance UK

Steve Clifford was the general director of the Evangelical Alliance UK from April 2009 to December 2019. His innovation and leadership have helped shape some of the UK church's biggest national campaigns.

Steve's previous roles have included chair of the Hope 08 campaign and the international youth festival Soul Survivor. He also served as an Evangelical Alliance and a Spring Harvest board member, where he chaired Soul in the City London and March for Jesus International. He worked as a teacher in the 1980s before leaving to work with the church in 1985, church planting and running leadership and discipleship teams.

Steve believes passionately in the church as an agent for change in our country, and is excited by all of the opportunities for the church to present the good news of Jesus in words and action.

Steve currently attends a church in west London. He is married to Ann, has a son, Jake, a daughter, Jordan, and three grandchildren.

Yemi Adedeji

Director, One People Commission at the Evangelical Alliance UK

Nigerian-born Rev Canon Yemi Adedeji is an ordained priest of the Anglican Church and a pentecostal pastor at Redeemed Christian Church of God Jesus House London. Canon Yemi is a former model, a consultant, leadership coach, author, pastor and speaker, with a passion to help leaders, churches and organisations develop deeper relationships.

He is currently serving as the director of the One People Commission at the Evangelical Alliance UK where he helps UK churches and Christian charities advance from the early stages of diversity into authentic inclusion and integration.

Yemi is also an associate director of HOPE Together, a hub for church mission and evangelism, and global ambassador at Compassion UK, where he helps to raise sponsors to release children from poverty.

Yemi is a regular BBC London commentator and a governor at the London School of Theology. He is married to Simi, a magistrate and property law professional. They are blessed with four daughters.

Acknowledgements

In producing this resource book, we recognise the profound influence of so many, some of whom continue to work alongside us, others who have gone before, building relationships and modelling a commitment to unity across the evangelical community.

Pastor Agu Irukwu and Bishop Wilton Powell who challenged us on our commitment to unity.

Matt Summerfield who called the Evangelical Alliance council to repentance for forgetting that the unity we talked about needed to reflect the vibrant ethnic diversity of the UK church.

Philip Mohabir (a missionary from Guyana) who started the African and Caribbean Evangelical Alliance (ACEA) in the 1980s and laid the foundation for so much we benefit from today.

Dr Tani Omideyi, the first BAME chair of the Evangelical Alliance council and board.

Joel Edwards, general secretary of ACEA, who later became general director of the Evangelical Alliance.

Hugh Osgood and Bishop Jo Aldred, pioneers in building bridges across ethnic expressions.

Those who have helped to shape the One People Commission, including many who continue to support and serve the OPC until this day:

Pastor Modupe Afolabi, Rev Celia Apeagyei-Collins, Rev Kingsley Appiagyei, Rev Gavin Calver, Bishop Donald Bolt, Rev Daniel Chae, Rev David Coffey, Pastor Samuel Cueva, Rev Jonathan Edwards, Pastor Omawami Efaeye, Roger Forster, Ruth Gilson, Rev John Glass, Pastor Surekha Hulugalle, Rev Dr Paul Jinadu, Dr David Landrum, Chine McDonald, Pastor Jonathan Oloyede, Rev Obafemi Omisade, John Partington, Bishop Delroy Powell, Bishop Tedroy Powell, Pastor Manoj Raithatha, Bishop Mike Royal, Rev John Risbridger, Pastor Chrishanthy Sathiyaraj, Bishop Keith Sinclair, Rev David Shosanya, Rev Roger Sutton, Sarah Riseley, Pastor Steve Uppal, Rachel Westcott, the late Dr Tayo Adeyemi, Rev Samson Awak-Essien, Rev Kofi Banful, Pastor Girma Bishaw, Rev Lyndon Bowring, Bishop Eric Brown, Rev Marcia Da Costa, Bishop John Francis, Ashraf Farahat, Pastor Wien Fung, Rev Namjin Kim, Bishop Wayne Malcolm,

Pastor Blair Mundell, Rev Nims Obunge, Pastor Omawumi Efueye, Pastor Ade Omooba, Rev Siew Huat Ong, Pastor David Oyedepo, Bishop Wilton Powell, Bishop Lee Rayfield, Rev Matt Summerfield, Rev Mike Talbot, Apostle Alfred Williams.

Special thanks to those who have worked to make this resource book possible.

Lucy Olofinjana, who worked serving the One People Commission in its early days and drew up the 'Lessons from the Journey,' which became the inspiration for this book and is included as a summary at the end.

Rachael Heffer, who conducted numerous interviews, wrote up many of the personal reflections and project-managed the book.

Jo Frost, our director of communications and membership, who inspired and challenged us every step of the way.

Eve Paterson and Naomi Osinnowo, who conducted interviews and wrote up many of the personal reflections.

Sarah Fisher, whose design and creativity always amazes us.

Catherine Butcher who worked on our rough manuscripts.

Tim Coysh, an exceptional designer who oversaw the design and production of the book.

Cassie Johnson who, with great patience, has served the One People Commission and typed up and printed more drafts than we care to count.

Israel Olofinjana, David Hilborn, Manoj Raithatha, and Tani Omideyi who kindly reviewed the manuscript.

To all those who were willing to make their contribution through personal reflections, your honesty, wisdom and encouragements have taken this resource to another level. Joe Aldred, Richard Anniss, Celia Apeagyei-Collins, Nicky Brown, Anne Calver, Ann Clifford, Roy Crowne, O'Neil Dennis, Andy Frost, Les Isaac OBE, Shantelle Johnson, Preethy Kurian, Israel Olofinjana, Tani Omideyi, Anu Omideyi, Manoj Raithatha, David Wise.

Foreword

PASTOR AGU IRUKWU

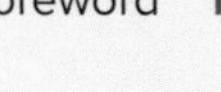

Pastor Agu Irukwu

Pastor Agu is a law graduate from the University of Warwick, a barrister and former investment banker. He was ordained a pastor in August 1993 and took over as senior pastor of Jesus House in April 1994, two months after it was birthed. He also serves as chairman of the board of trustees and head of the executive council of the Redeemed Christian Church of God in the UK. In 2017 he was appointed the pentecostal president of Churches Together in England (CTE) for the period of October 2017 to September 2021.

A meeting of the Evangelical Alliance's council in 2010 is an event that few attendees will forget, as God spoke through Bishop Wilton Powell OBE and myself about the plans He had for this great organisation. I remember we had reservations about sharing what we felt God had laid on our hearts, not because we were uncertain, but because it would lead to, if acted upon, a long, challenging journey that would require much adjustment and sacrifice.

At the time, black and ethnic minority churches were doing impactful work in different spheres in the UK. To pinpoint London, as an example, these churches were at the forefront of the expansion of the body of Christ. But they had limited representation at the highest levels of the Evangelical Alliance, the organisation that represents the evangelical church of the land.

The African and Caribbean Evangelical Alliance (ACEA), founded by Guyanese missionary Philip Mohabir in 1984, was a national umbrella organisation for black-majority churches in the UK which operated separately to, but with the support of, the Evangelical Alliance. When the ACEA disbanded in 2010, there were legitimate concerns around who would represent these Christian communities going forward.

God made it clear at that council meeting: it was time for the Evangelical Alliance to go deeper and wider, by becoming a dedicated voice for, and fostering even closer relationships with, the UK's ethnically diverse evangelical church. Interestingly, God did not share His vision with Wilton and me alone; He had laid it on the hearts of many of the leaders in attendance, and we realised that if we flowed with the Spirit of God, He would lead us to something completely new, something that would transform the nations. But if we didn't heed the Spirit, we would miss the season and would be left with no option but to await another. We give thanks to the Spirit of God that it went well.

I commend Steve Clifford, who grabbed the bull by the horns in 2010, only a year after succeeding Rev Joel Edwards, the Evangelical Alliance's first black pentecostal general director. It couldn't have been easy trying to change established structures and practices, and lead the journey towards greater ethnic integration within the UK church. Indeed, he opened the doors to those who are different in expression, culture, liturgy, and a million and one other things. He brought ethnic minority churches into the centre of the Evangelical Alliance. Steve was incredible in how he embraced the work that needed to be done, and his legacy will be demonstrating that ethnic diversity is good, and unity is possible.

Canon Yemi Adedeji was in the body for such a time as that. As a person from an ethnic minority in the UK, Yemi understood differences and nuances in cultures – and there are many. He teamed up with Steve and has played a pivotal role in transforming the Evangelical Alliance to what it is today. He has brought in the zest of the ethnic minority churches.

I recall both Steve and Yemi visiting numerous ethnic minority leaders and simply listening to them. Steve and Yemi did an exceptional job listening, and I wholeheartedly applaud them for their listening ear. The Evangelical Alliance's One People Commission (OPC) was established in 2012 as a result of those vital conversations that took place. And this network of Christian and church leaders, which was set up to celebrate ethnic diversity while promoting unity, has done and continues to do an amazing work in integrating the body.

This resource book, a testimony and a witness to what God is doing in our country through His church, brings information and shares experiences. It brings a breath of knowledge that has been garnered by Steve, Yemi and the other contributors. There's an old saying that African leaders use: "You don't buy experience in the market; somebody has travailed." The fruits of the pain they went through in building what they have built is in these pages, as the OPC seeks to equip others and share tools, and as we work together for a more united church for the sake of the gospel.

I am personally grateful and encouraged that they have opened up, and I believe their honesty, practical tips and calls to reflect will equip, position and strengthen the church to do what it is designed to do: reach out and work together to make Jesus known. One of the things I love about what is happening at the Evangelical Alliance is how we bring our gifts and graces to the table: some of us have an incredibly deep theological understanding, while others have a passion for prayer, and a bold, outrageous faith, where we believe God for everything. At the Evangelical Alliance, this all mixes together, iron sharpens iron, and this book points to what is happening and what could be, as God's people come together in complete unity.

We need a tool of this sort, for no church has arrived yet. But I see a number of churches that are on the way and are at various stages in the journey. A lot of the churches were closed up; there was no exchange of pulpits or ideas. It has dawned on a number of us that there has to be change. First comes the realisation that is birthed by the Spirit of God that a particular model has reached the end, and if you do not change, you are going to be treading water. At leadership level I have seen, and continue to see, different people exploring new avenues to break out of that cave. And there have been different levels of success. Steve and Yemi, and Yemi and Gavin Calver, are vivid images of this change.

My church is no exception. It's on the journey too. Some years ago, the congregation was predominantly one Nigerian tribe; I was the only Nigerian who was not part of that tribe. Gradually, other people of other Nigerian tribes joined Jesus House, and over time Caribbean people have found their home at the church and have joined our leadership team.

Now people from Brazilian and other African backgrounds are part of our community. Nevertheless, we still seek a quantum leap in ethnic integration. Our congregants all look alike; it's only when they speak that you recognise the difference. The quantum leap is when people who don't look like us join the fellowship. Many predominantly white churches find themselves in the same position, making room for people who don't have the same skin colour as them.

So, as we strive for greater ethnic unity, I hope and pray that the book will have the breath of God on it. I pray it brings healing to those who have suffered as a result of what was, and there are many who did. I pray it brings encouragement as we see what the Lord has done. I pray it helps us overcome the hindrances that stop us from moving towards ethnic unity – fear of the unknown, a lack of political will, complacency – and ignites in us the desire to go for it, knowing that there will be cost involved.

Introduction: The Why

STEVE CLIFFORD

As we sat down in my west London home in 2011, little did I know the journey we were about to embark upon. Over the next three hours Rev Canon Yemi Adedeji was to provide me with my very first in-depth induction into the life of the ethnic minority churches in the UK. I had been involved in church leadership for decades. I'd had the privilege of bringing leadership to national initiatives such as March for Jesus, Soul in the City, and Hope 08, but I was about to realise that I was still living with major areas of ignorance. While many of these initiatives had involved the ethnic minority churches, I came to see I had major blind spots and that we had only managed to scratch the surface of God's heart for the integration of His people across the wide spectrum of the ethnic backgrounds which make up the church in the UK.

Yemi and I were meeting as a direct result of what had happened at our council meeting on 15 September 2010. The council was made up of around 80 men and women, senior leaders from across the spectrum of the evangelical world. These were leaders in churches, heads of agencies, and key influencers in areas of business, politics, education and media. We met twice a year to discuss, feedback on and shape the work of the Evangelical Alliance, as well as to explore key issues influencing the Christian and, indeed, the wider world. The focus of the council was unity, but I had not been prepared for what I now believe was a historic moment for the Evangelical Alliance and for the church here in the UK. Early in the afternoon, Bishop Wilton Powell of the Church of God of Prophecy and Pastor Agu Irukwu, the UK leader of the Redeemed Christian Church of God and senior pastor of Jesus House, addressed the council. Their challenge was simple, but profound: if we were serious about unity, it had to be a unity which crossed all ethnic expressions of the church and refused to accept any divides. Here was a call for unity in the midst of diversity – a unity as expressed in the great John 17 prayer of Jesus. As they took their seats, the room fell silent in what I could only describe as a 'God moment'.

The council responded to the challenge, kneeling together in prayer and calling out to God. There was a recognition that so much of our unity to this point, whether nationally or within the context of our local congregations, had overlooked the vibrant diversity of the UK church.

That moment proved to be the first step of a personal journey, but also one which had significant impact on the Evangelical Alliance. It was also to have an impact on churches and organisations across the country. I'm so grateful to God for the prophetic words which were brought to us back in 2010. I've been enriched, encouraged and challenged as we have attempted to work through the implications of that significant moment. I have developed new friendships and experienced the rich tapestry of the wonderfully diverse expressions of the body of Christ here in the UK. It's a journey that continues to this day, working alongside leaders in the One People Commission. This was started in 2013 to rise to be an organisation which reflects the ethnic diversity of the UK church and asks the question, how do we need to change? We are aware that there is still much to be done.

In this resource book we will attempt to capture some of the lessons we have learnt and the mistakes we have made at times. This book reflects the journey of an organisation, the Evangelical Alliance, but also of two friends, Yemi Adedeji and me, Steve Clifford, as we have travelled together, discovering what unity across ethnicity means in practice. We are still learning. There is still ground to be taken, but this is our offering. We include contributions from others who have embarked on this journey; we seek to acknowledge all that they have experienced and learnt, but we recognise that this book is written through the lens of a white British and a black Nigerian leader. While the One People Commission does gather leaders from a wide range of ethnic backgrounds, we are aware that in writing this book, we are bringing our own insights and challenges based on our particular ethnic backgrounds.

We also recognise the limitations of language, which can fuel preconceptions. Terms like BME (black minority ethnic) or BAME (black, Asian and minority ethnic) can seem dehumanising. The term 'people of colour' used to describe non-white people, suggests that white is not a colour. We have opted to use BAME and 'ethnic minority churches' to describe the rich variety of non-white people who make up the British population, but in doing so, we recognise that assumptions cannot be based on skin colour in multi-cultural Britain, and 'ethnic minority' puts the emphasis on people being in the minority when, for example in cities such as London, it is white people who are in the minority in terms of church attendance.

Why is ethnic integration important?

In John chapter 17, a few hours before He will hang on the cross, Jesus is with His close friends. The crowds have gone and He is praying for them. But He is also praying for us: "...those who will believe in me through their message" (John 17:20). His prayer is simple yet profoundly challenging (verse 23): "I in them and you in me – so that they may be brought to complete unity. Then the world will know that you sent me and have loved them even as you have loved me."

Put simply, unity amongst God's people, and I suggest particularly as it impacts on our ethnic diversity, is important because it's on God's agenda. It's vital to Him. It seems that this unity or oneness He has called us to carries a missional imperative: "then the world will know...". This kind of unity is beyond doctrinal agreement or mutual appreciation and love. It seems, as we read the prayer of Jesus, that we are called to participate in the unity of the godhead, out of which we discover our true identity and a unity in love, in truth, and in mission. It's a unity that is impossible without God. Pragmatism is not enough. We pursue this unity, not because of political correctness, demographic trends or church growth and missional success; we do it because it's right and it's in God's word. It reflects God's heart and brings a challenge to each of us in our local churches or our national organisations. It might well involve repentance; it certainly requires a change of direction.

The issue of race and racism continues to be an issue of contention and conflict, not only in the UK but also around the world, even in God's church. We live in an age of increasing fragmentation, as we separate ourselves into self-defined groups built around age, ethnicity, culture, class, wealth, educational achievement and profession. In fact, for many, individualism reigns supreme: "I'm the centre of my universe." The prayer of Jesus, the teaching of scripture, and the model of the early church, will not allow us to get away with such an approach. God is calling His people to challenge the spirit of our age, to be truly counter-cultural and to live another way.

What's our response?

Jesus prayed so we don't need to worry. We can relax. Not so! The teaching of scripture and our everyday experience of life makes it clear we can't relax. It seems we may have been brought to "complete unity," but there's something to be maintained, developed and protected. So many of Paul's letters focus on this theme. In the book of Ephesians, Paul goes to some length spelling out our response.

"As a prisoner for the Lord, then, I urge you to live a life worthy of the calling you have received. Be completely humble and gentle; be patient, bearing with one another in love. Make every effort to keep the unity of the Spirit through the bond of peace. There is one body and one Spirit, just as you were called to one hope when you were called; one Lord, one faith, one baptism; one God and Father of all, who is over all and through all and in all" (Ephesians 4:1-6).

Paul is determined that we recognise our 'oneness'. He says "one" seven times in just two verses: one body, one Spirit, one hope, one Lord, one faith, one baptism, one God and Father. Paul has begun with an exhortation, perhaps reflecting some of the difficulties in the church to which he is writing. He exhorts them to "live a life worthy of the calling you have received". In other words, be true to who you are. Then he gets very specific: "Be completely humble and gentle; be patient, bearing with one another in love". It sounds like a great way for Christians to relate to each other. This is where Paul is leading us: "Make every effort to keep the unity of the Spirit in the bond of peace". Paul is giving a strong directive to these first century Christians. Their unity was not an optional extra; they were required to "make every effort" to keep, maintain and sustain this unity. Paul makes it abundantly clear: there is work to be done in order to maintain what Jesus had prayed for and then, through His death and resurrection, had made a spiritual reality. This book is designed to help us 21st century Christians as we respond to this challenge today.

So it seems our 'oneness' is not in doubt, but it needs looking after, nurturing and protecting. Unity has to be worked at. Thank God for the unity that Jesus prayed for and Paul contended for. It's not a unity which demands uniformity, but a unity in the midst of amazing diversity. Thank God He is not asking us to become the same as each other. We are called to oneness and yet we look and sound so different. We will experience God as our Lord and Saviour, but we will pray, worship, teach scripture and model leadership in a multitude of different ways.

So, we pray that this resource book will provide a helpful aid as we explore our unity as expressed across all ethnic expressions.

What holds us back?

This resource book has been written for all who have a heart for unity, particularly those who carry responsibility in the context of local churches and organisations that are working across cities, regions or nations. As we explore different practical steps to better express our unity, it is helpful to recognise different pressures and influences that could hold us back. Each needs to be addressed if we are to take seriously Paul's exhortation to "make every effort to keep the unity of the Spirit".

Different worlds

As I began my exploration, I quickly realised that I had lived for decades within my own particular church world and was pretty much oblivious to so much that was going on in other worlds. Enormous conferences and prayer gatherings attracted thousands of people. Books and CDs from other parts of the church were sold in tens of thousands. International ministers, who I had never heard of, travelled the world, and lived in my city. There were also enormous buildings owned and filled by mainly African and Caribbean people. I realised that I had lived in my world for too long and, if I was serious about unity, I had to learn about these other worlds and allow my world to be stretched and, at times, challenged.

Bias and stereotypes

Living in different worlds, it is easy for bias to exist unchallenged, suspicion to grow and stereotypes to flourish. At their very worst these stereotypes can be racist and require repentance. As Yemi and I have spoken over the last few years, we have begun to recognise the preconceived ideas that so many of us have lived with:

- "Black church leaders talk about money all the time"; "white church leaders don't talk about money enough".
- "White churches are declining"; "black churches are prospering".
- "Black leadership is hierarchical"; "white leaders don't lead".
- "White churches are soft on moral behaviour"; "black churches are legalistic".
- "White churches are all theology and no experience"; "black churches are all experience and no theology".
- "Black leaders can't be depended upon – they are always late if they turn up at all"; "white

> leaders love forming committees, stifling spontaneity and perhaps quenching the Spirit".

These stereotypes act as barriers, presuppositions that undermine trust and make it difficult to develop relationships.

Superior attitudes

Stereotyping can bring with it an attitude that impacts on how we relate to each other. Paul makes it clear: "...do not think of yourself more highly than you ought, but rather think of yourself with sober judgment" (Romans 12:3). It's so easy for leaders to develop a superior attitude to brothers and sisters in Christ, particularly if their expression of church or ministry is different. Often we might not even realise that we hold these attitudes, that our way of doing things is the correct way, and that others have got it wrong.

Painful experiences from the past

Over the journey of the last few years, I've heard numerous heart-breaking stories of how ethnic minority brothers and sisters have been treated within the church, and I've recognised how my own behaviour in the past has not nurtured genuine partnerships and respectful relationships. For example, I've worked on plans with other white leaders, forgetting to bring my brothers and sisters from BAME churches in at the start of projects to help shape the strategies from the beginning. I've had to say sorry, and I'm grateful that these brothers and sisters have been willing to extend grace and forgiveness. Pain from the past will create barriers to the future unless addressed.

Miscommunications

In the coming pages we will explore communication and how easy it is to misunderstand each other. It can be particularly damaging when we go away from a meeting thinking we have agreed something, only to realise that not everyone in the room has heard or agreed the same things. When such events take place it's easy for leaders to conclude "we tried and it just didn't work".

No ethnic minorities in our area

There are some parts of the UK where the village, town or even city is overwhelmingly monocultural. However, the principles within this resource can be adapted to explore unity which crosses other divides, such as class and social-economic status. Sadly, the church across the UK still has much to learn if it is to avoid simply reaching the middle and higher educated classes.

Busyness

As we will see, relationships are a key to this expression of unity. However, leaders, whether in churches or organisations, are living busy lives. Building trusting relationships takes time and effort. It demands making a priority for meeting up for tea or coffee, finding out about each other – our lives, not just our ministries. It means making the effort to attend other people's churches or events without the expectation of participation, but simply to learn and receive.

Fundamentally, it's simply not a priority

Some leaders, either intentionally or by default, have come to the conclusion that, with everything else that's going on around their church, their organisation, their life, this just isn't a priority. To those leaders I would say:

- perhaps God would wish these opportunities for relationships to be a blessing rather than a drain;
- by taking just a few small steps you could reap great rewards;
- perhaps there is someone else in your leadership team who could be mandated to develop these relationships;
- perhaps you might examine your priorities in the light of scripture.

This is our future

The book of Revelation gives us a snapshot of the age to come: "After this I looked, and there before me was a great multitude that no one could count, from every nation, tribe, people and language, standing before the throne and before the Lamb. They were wearing white robes and were holding palm branches in their hands. And they cried out in a loud voice: 'Salvation belongs to our God, who sits on the throne, and to the Lamb' (Revelation 7:9-10).

This resource book is a call to action, a call to unity in the midst of amazing diversity, a call to include ourselves on God's agenda here and now, in the full knowledge it will be fully expressed in the age to come.

At a time when across the world walls are being built to reinforce racial divides, God is calling us, His church, to use those bricks that make up the walls to build bridges and so provide a prophetic challenge to the world. I thank God for the ethnic minority churches here in the UK. I believe they are a gift to the historically indigenous population. I'm convinced we need each other if we are to see the UK reached with the transforming power of the gospel. This is a time for us to "make every effort", to build relationships, to honour each other, to learn from each other, and to be enriched as we celebrate our oneness in Christ.

1

Developing Relationships

How do we develop genuine relationships with people who are different from us?

STEVE CLIFFORD

What's the secret?

In recent years and in various settings, leaders from all kinds of backgrounds have asked me a very similar question: "When it comes to working with the ethnic minority churches, how do you do it?" This question is particularly relevant for leaders of agencies and ministries wishing to serve the evangelical community, as we estimate that between 20 and 25 per cent of evangelical Christians are from a BAME background, and in some cities the proportion will be a lot higher. But similar questions are being faced by numerous church leaders across the country, whether it's ethnic minority churches looking to reach out to their wider community where the majority of the population is white, or indigenous white-led churches wanting to reflect the ethnic diversity of their area and welcome BAME Christians and those who could find faith.

When I'm asked the question, my answer is pretty much always the same: "There is no secret." There could be principles to learn from each other's experiences, but there is no 'silver bullet'. The key is relationships, or put another way building friendships. These kinds of relationship require time and effort; they don't develop overnight – they require intentional commitment. It means prioritising people before any suggestion of a project.

For me, what happened at our 2010 council meeting, mentioned in the introduction, was to have a profound impact. I knew I had to respond. So, following up with some wise advice from Pastor Agu Irukwu and Bishop Wilton Powell, who had brought the challenge to the council, I embarked on a year of coffees, teas, pizzas and curries, beginning to make contact and build relationships with a wide cross section of the BAME church leaders. This involved me getting out of my office and making the journey, having my eyes opened to just what was going on in parts of the church I knew so little about. I discovered God was at work and He was doing the business of heaven in some amazing ways here in the UK. Alongside these various one-to-one meetings, I began to attend various events and conferences; not first and foremost with the intention of speaking (although I would often be asked to bring a greeting), but to experience first-hand what God was doing, and to learn.

One family

We should not underestimate how the first-century Christians struggled with the issue of race. Until this time YHWH belonged to one racial group, the Jews. But it seemed as if God was opening Himself to everyone. The Holy Spirit was messing up all their preconceived ideas as to how things should be. It's amazing to me that these early Christian leaders took so long to realise the implications of all that Jesus had achieved through His life, death and resurrection – God working out the great promises made to Abraham in Genesis 12:3: "...all peoples on earth will be blessed through you". Why could they not appreciate the significance of the day of Pentecost, the birth of the church, but also the reversal of Babel (Genesis 11) as crowds from so many parts of the world heard and understood the apostles in their own language. Surely what we now know as the great commission, Jesus' last instructions to His disciples, made it clear they were to make disciples of all nations. Why did it need Peter's encounter with Cornelius in Acts 10, or indeed the council of Jerusalem in Acts 15, following Paul's first missionary journey, to establish the principle that the gospel was for everyone, regardless of their background and without the requirements to become a Jew?

The book of Galatians is written to a church facing conflict. Some in the church wanted the non-Jewish Christians to adopt the old ways, relying on the Jewish law. Paul is adamant in his denunciation of this approach: "There is neither Jew nor Gentile, neither slave nor free, nor is there male and female, for you are all one in Christ Jesus" (Galatians 3:28). Paul goes on to make clear that our faith in Jesus Christ causes us to enter a new family, regardless of ethnicity, religious backgrounds, social status or gender. We are part of the family. We are clothed in Christ. We are one in Christ. Because of this truth, we share our Father in heaven; we have the amazing privilege of praying "our Father". Because we are part of the same family, regardless of racial background, we are brothers and sisters in Christ Jesus. As we explore relationships within this chapter, we do so with this revelation as our foundation. We are family. The words of Jesus echo in our ears: "By this everyone will know that you are my disciples, if you love one another" (John 13:35). This is a family marked out, not by rules or regulations, but by love.

Going deeper

Relationships come in all kinds of shapes and sizes, from the relatively superficial, to our good friends, and perhaps a few that are in-depth, vulnerable and life-changing. While the importance of the superficial should not be underestimated, if we are serious about unity in the family of God, we must be prepared to go deeper at least with some. Over the years my family, living as an extended household, has had people from numerous different nations living with us, including at one stage, Jackie, Yemi's

daughter. We have relished the rich diversity of culture this has exposed us to. An Asian guy, whose family were from a Muslim background in Pakistan, lived with us for two years. His family wanted to arrange a marriage for him. As a young Yorkshireman by birth and accent, he wasn't keen on this proposal. We've had two Iranian female students living with us too, including us in their traditional festivals and celebrations, such as purchasing goldfish for the Persian New Year! And, of course, our son, Jake, married Asha Chhaganlall, who has a Mauritian heritage, so we are now a mixed-race family. Moving from the superficial requires an investment of ourselves, our time, energy, finances and emotional capacity. Here are some principles which will help in this process.

Attitudes matter

If we are serious about developing relationships that cross ethnic divides, it's important that we start by getting our attitude right. As Paul told the Philippians: "Do nothing out of selfish ambition or vain conceit. Rather, in humility value others above yourselves" (Philippians 2:3). Humility reflects an attitude of heart which says, "I want to learn, I don't know it all, I have my understanding, but I could be wrong." Humility means we approach relationships asking questions rather than making strong statements. For me, one of the delights of recent years has been working alongside Dr Tani Omideyi, who is senior pastor of Liverpool Lighthouse and is now the chair of the Evangelical Alliance board. We speak regularly, either face to face or on the phone, and a similar pattern has emerged. First we catch up on family and church life, and then we pray for each other and the work God has called us to. Then the conversation moves on as we ask each other questions and I gain wisdom and insight from Tani's extensive experience of church leadership and ministry within multicultural churches and beyond. Conversations such as this, however they take place, require us to make sure that we are listening well and that we do our best to get inside each other's worlds. Sometimes we can use the same words but mean something very different.

Stepping out of our comfort zones

Many of us have a world around us that has become familiar; we feel comfortable and safe in it. If we are to build relationships and ultimately churches and ministries, which are genuinely ethnically integrated, we have to be prepared to step out of our comfort zones and experience other people's worlds.

A few years ago my wife Ann and I established an annual garden party, reflecting a quintessential British culture. Ann got out her granny's tea service; cream teas, sandwiches and cakes were served. We invited friends, church and organisational leaders from across the evangelical world. Our aim was to start mixing friends from different ethnic expressions of the church, including indigenous white leaders. It was at the end of one of these garden parties that

Pastor Chrishanthy Sathiyaraj, a church leader from the Sri Lankan community, who had lived in the UK for years, reflected with sadness that this was the very first time she had been inside a white British person's home, let alone experienced a garden party and a strange drink known as 'elderflower'.

Over the last few years, I have found myself experiencing first-hand being one of the few, and on occasion the only, white faces in a room of thousands of people. Of course, this is the usual experience of many BAME Christians as they visit a white-majority church. Stepping out of my comfort zone has taken me into meetings within the UK conducted in Korean, Portuguese, French, Romanian, Tamil and Spanish. I've experienced worship, prayer and public ministry conducted in amazingly diverse ways: from the exuberant and loud pentecostal traditions of some churches to more liturgical and formal styles. I've also visited churches working hard to express a diversity of cultural styles within their gatherings, aiming to reflect the multicultural nature of their community. I thank God there is not just one way of expressing ourselves as a church. As I have overcome my own preferences, I've been enriched, blessed and encouraged by the diverse expressions of the church we find here in the UK.

I confess, there have been a few occasions when I have been caught out. Arriving at a meeting expecting the service to be conducted in English, only to find it isn't. Preaching with an interpreter can radically impact on your message. Expecting a two-hour service and finding it's still going after three can impact on your plans for the rest of the day. Once I arrived to preach at a church on the day that the clocks went back an hour. The pastor said he wished he'd invited me on a different day, as his BAME church had a flexible approach to time on any Sunday, but on this occasion, the congregation weren't all present until about 1pm. On at least one occasion, I desperately needed Yemi's guidance to understand the model of prayer and ministry that was taking place as it was outside my previous experience.

Learning from the way others pray has been a deeply humbling experience. In recent years hundreds of South Korean Christians have come to the UK to pray for us. They pay to come in their annual holidays, often sleeping on church floors as their prayer teams move around the country to pray with and for Christians here.

Stepping out of our comfort zones becomes very practical when it comes to social interaction. I've noticed in social settings, whether at the end of a church meeting, at a party, or some kind of celebration, how we often stay within the comfort of our own ethnic group. Being willing to walk across the room, intentionally overcoming any sense of awkwardness, and engaging relationally, is a discipline we need to teach ourselves and our congregations. Incidentally, as a white man walking across the room, I have learned that my opening question should never be: "Where do you come from?" Such a question makes an assumption that the person, because they have a different skin colour to mine, was born outside the UK. Having exchanged names and pleasantries, a question such as: "Where do your family originate from?" can widen the conversation and allow me to explore my own heritage as a Yorkshireman.

Honest conversations

Ben Lindsay, a black church leader leading a majority-white church, has written a really helpful book *We Need to Talk About Race* (SPCK Publishing, July 2019). He focuses particularly on the experience of black Christians within majority-white churches in the UK. Drawing on his own experience and those he has spoken with, he argues among other things that we must be prepared as the title suggests to "to talk about race". Of course, these conversations are not easy and should not be embarked upon too soon in a relationship. Trust needs to be built; the relationships need to have gone deeper before talking about difficulties. These conversations are not easy because no white person wants to appear racist, so there is a fear they could say something wrong. At the same time, for an ethnic minority person, they don't want to appear overly sensitive, self-indulgent or as a victim. Having these kinds of conversations requires us to be brave, to listen well, and white people in particular need to work hard not to become defensive or dismissive.

What we talk about

What we talk about will vary from one person to the next. One of the mistakes white Christians can make is to assume that all ethnic minority people's experience is the same or that all ethnic minority churches are the same. The worldview and experience of Chinese, Korean, Caribbean and African Christians varies greatly as do individual experiences within these ethnic groups. These honest conversations need to take time so personal stories are heard, so we appreciate the joys and pains of life experienced here in the UK. Some will want to express the racism they have been exposed to both outside and, sadly, inside the church. They might want to explain the privileges they have been denied.

I wouldn't be honest if I didn't admit that some of my conversations have been personally challenging as things were pointed out to me to which I had been blind. Chatting over coffees and teas, I have been brought face to face with my own pattern of behaviour, which I realise can in fact be damaging to the unity that I thought I had been promoting. I can recall the numerous occasions I had been part of a team that came up with a great vision and decided at a later stage to connect with black and Asian leaders, sharing our brilliant plans with them. But as was graciously explained to me, this was not real unity. These leaders wanted to be part of the conversation and the planning leading up to these events and initiatives, not included at the last minute to rubber stamp what we (the white leaders) had already decided.

Sometimes Yemi has taken me aside and explained how my actions have marginalised the BAME contribution, leaving key players out of the decision-making process. At times I've explained to Yemi how his leadership style can be misinterpreted. The Nigerian style is to give a strong lead, using statements like "I must..." when, to encourage collective responsibility, it would be better to use the word "we", thus changing the emphasis from a personal battle to a joint enterprise. Yemi has challenged me about the language I've used at times, and we've talked about the loud, assertive tone, which is normal in Nigerian culture, but which can seem aggressive in a white Christian context. These conversations, which have challenged us to change, have been possible because we respect each other. It can be easy to respond defensively or to try to sort everything out. Instead, it is better to listen well and to seek to understand, rather than bring clarification, which can often sound like self-justification.

I've had to be willing to be made uncomfortable, facing up to the realities of what's really happening in my own life and in the wider UK church, and recognising the work that still needs to be done. I've heard heart-breaking stories, such as that of a church in the UK locking beakers away from a black children's creche for fear of contamination; of new converts turned away from baptism for fear that they might be illegal immigrants and of missionaries coming to the UK from the Caribbean, Asia and Africa, facing persecution and prejudice within our churches. And these aren't stories from the 1960s but from 21st-century Britain. These conversations need to go further, looking at the social issues that are important to BAME communities. For white Christians that might throw up some surprises.

A few years ago, as a team, the Evangelical Alliance invited a group of ethnic minority leaders to advise us on the social and political issues they were concerned about, to which the Evangelical Alliance might give some profile. I confess I didn't expect the list that emerged; issues around property were top of the list.

It resulted in us as a team beginning to adjust our communications and advocacy work to reflect these concerns. I came out of the meeting knowing that, if we were serious about being the family of God, it was vital that issues that concerned one section of the family should become a concern of the whole family. The silence from white expressions of church on some of these important issues could be interpreted as apathy, or more seriously, as assent. So, issues of gun and knife crime, overrepresentation of certain ethnicities in the prison population, and the inadequate provision of mental health services to black and ethnic minorities needs to be the whole church's concern, the focus of our public and private prayer and, where appropriate, action.

As we are engaged in these conversations, we will discover the reality of our differences. Yes, we are one in Christ Jesus. This is our spiritual identity, but the 'colour blindness' that some Christians aspire to is not a positive thing as it fails to recognise the amazing diversity of the body of Christ: the joys, pains, fears and experiences of the 21st-century church here in the UK. Relationships are built as we hear each other's stories, both positive and negative, and not only acknowledge our differences, but learn to celebrate them.

How do we need to change?

As we, the Evangelical Alliance, responded to the challenge we felt God had brought to us, we realised there was a key question we needed to be brave enough to ask: "How do we need to change?" If we were to ask others to consider change, then we needed to face the question ourselves. The coming chapters will give you some insight as to our response. Although we haven't arrived, we have made some significant steps along the journey. For other organisations and churches, the response to this question will vary, but the willingness to change is essential. Truly integrated expressions of church or ministries will not simply happen because of our good intentions, although that's a good starting place. The journey to integration starts by a recognition of the diversity of the family of God, and a desire to see that expressed. The journey takes place as we work intentionally at inclusion. Not satisfied with the status quo, we commit ourselves to learning and to change. As change takes hold, we discover that it becomes embedded in the life, culture, relationships and structures of the organisation and we begin to become integrated. Leaders face the challenge of taking their churches or ministries with them. Wholescale major change overnight could prove disastrous, so wisdom is needed. Initially, this might mean a few small steps and changes of behaviour and practice. But, as one leader of a majority Nigerian church shared with his congregation, "If we don't change we are finished." He knew that they needed to adjust how they expressed themselves as church so they could connect more effectively with the diverse community around them.

Manoj Raithatha

Manoj Raithatha has been a secondary school teacher, a Bafta award-winning TV writer and a successful property entrepreneur. Following God's miraculous intervention in his son's illness in 2008, Manoj committed his life to Jesus Christ. Since then, he has been involved in various ministries including the oversight of the South Asian Forum team at the Evangelical Alliance and establishing the publishing house Instant Apostle. Manoj is pastor of Pinner Baptist Church. He is of South Asian background and is passionate about equipping and releasing people from across the ethnic and age spectrum to realise their potential in Christ. He works to encourage South Asian church leaders to work more collaboratively with the wider church in the collective mission of God.

Developing relationships isn't rocket science, but it often comes at a cost and with effort. This is especially the case in the midst of different cultures, traditions and expectations.

I am a South Asian leader and while I was living in a very affluent area of London, I felt called by God to work and minister in one of the poorest boroughs in London. Leaving a white-majority church, I found myself in Barking, in a predominantly African and Caribbean community. Many local people struggle with a lack of education, prospects and confidence. I quickly realised that I needed to do a lot of learning, personal growth and understanding of cultures outside of my own experience.

As a church leader, I have always sought to prioritise relationships, so I felt convinced that the key to better integration within the church, and with those on the margins, was to intentionally develop fruitful relationships. The truth is that this can be costly, fraught with challenges and exhausting, but nothing can supersede the joy of establishing a positive relationship with someone and seeing them flourish.

One day, while a friend was praying with me, he had a vivid picture from God of being at a wedding, walking around the reception tables and putting individual name cards on people's places. I immediately sensed through this picture that God was calling me to invest in people as individuals, which would lead to positive growth and investment in the kingdom. This radically enhanced my ministry and helped me develop principles I've lived by ever since.

First, I started by taking seriously the call for unity under the lordship of Jesus which is described in Ephesians 1. We are all His dearly beloved children, equal in the body of Christ, and second, we all have a unique story; when we stop to listen, it can be life-changing for our listeners as well as for us. Third, I recognised that, as leaders, we need to have humility and openness to change. Pausing to listen is time-consuming, but it allows us to understand people's cultural norms, how they view and inhabit the world. We will often need to adapt in order to be genuinely inclusive and loving to those who are different to ourselves, so we can't hold things too tightly.

Finally, relationships built on trust are the key to encouraging others to step into a new gifting or new roles. This has transformed the lives of many individuals within our church community who, by trusting me or other leaders and friends, have been willing to grasp a new opportunity. Whether it's reading, sharing their testimony, speaking, leading worship, or doing mission, their contribution adds to the richness of diversity, love and integration across the church.

Daniel, a black man in his 20s, is a brilliant example of this. I felt it right to prioritise time with Daniel, and over 18 months his growth has been exponential. After initially being hesitant to enter fully into the life of the church, Daniel has now joined the welcome team, invested in youth ministry, and has been voted in as a deacon. I'm so thankful for the way God uses us to build relationships, overcome ethnic divides, and bring about His kingdom plans in people's lives!

In my experience, whilst this investment in people groups and individuals is both biblical and godly, it can be messy. That's why it's so important that we keep no record of wrongs, forgive freely, and commit wholeheartedly to the long journey towards Christlikeness. We must release ourselves as leaders from fear or the desire to control and earnestly seek to be secure in Christ, for the glory of God and the growth of His kingdom.

Meals provide natural opportunities for building relationships. When we read the gospels, it soon becomes clear that Jesus intentionally allocated time to eat with people, and that these meals were about far more than just food. We see Him eat with His disciples at the last supper; with the multitudes at the feeding of the 5,000; with Levi the tax collector; and with Zacchaeus and others. Sharing a meal with someone always builds intimacy, and Jesus was clearly seeking to do this with all sorts of people. While they ate together, people had opportunities to experience Emmanuel, God with us, in a way they could relate to and understand – after all, what better way to demonstrate God incarnate than to share lunch.

Joe Aldred

Dr Joe Aldred is principal officer for pentecostal and multicultural relations from Churches Together in England, and a Bishop in the Church of God of Prophecy from the pentecostal tradition. He is a broadcaster as well as an ecumenist, providing 'Pause for Thought' for BBC Radio 4 and having regular slots on UCB radio. Bishop Joe has written a number of books, including *Respect*, about understanding Caribbean British Christianity, and *Thinking Outside the Box*.

Most people would agree that no two communities look the same. When it comes to black-majority churches, however, they can often be grouped together even though they are actually just as varied as all other church communities.

One of the core ways that I have learnt to develop relationships in my context has been between leaders of these different black-majority churches. Although there will be many similarities, there are also several key differences, especially between pentecostal and non-pentecostal expressions of church. The question for me has always been: "How do we develop a greater sense of unity among black-majority churches?"

Initially, we felt that the main hindrance to unity was a lack of connectedness through information. We began addressing the problem by creating a directory of black-majority and multicultural churches, which unfortunately, due to GDPR constraints, is no longer in use. We weren't aware of anything like this in existence, so the database definitely served a vital purpose for that season. But as useful as it had been, what the database simply couldn't do was replicate face-to-face contact.

Following the loss of the database, we realised that knowing all the relevant information about a church is not the same as genuinely knowing the people who make up that community. If we wanted greater unity then we needed to get people in the room, not just onto a database. That's where the Churches Together in England Pentecostal and Charismatic Forum has proved crucial for us. Every six months a gathering of church leaders from a variety of ethnic backgrounds, not just black-majority, has met to develop relationships, share information and ideas, and grow in unity together. The bi-annual forum has been vital in engaging leaders in what is happening at a national level, focusing them on the bigger picture beyond their own context.

Alongside this, I've also learnt that in all areas of church life, we need to address the theology behind our practices. Subsequently, in 2016 I helped to start a theological forum where papers were presented by voices who might otherwise not have been heard. The result was the publication of a book that directly focused on pentecostals and charismatics in Britain. In this way, we gave space, a platform, and the opportunity for collaboration between those who were theologically active in these communities, not just those in church leadership.

Throughout all of this, the biggest challenge I've come across is the idea that ethnicity should be subservient to Christian unity. On the contrary, I believe that the ethnicity of a community is hugely important to them and the church as a whole. By disregarding people's ethnicity completely, we risk devaluing or entirely losing their contribution to the UK church. There aren't easy solutions to this, but what I've learnt is that these communities, like all, must be based on openness, a continued desire to learn, and increasingly deepening relationships.

Despite the loss of our database, I still think that better information will transform the way we are unified as the church. By deepening relationships that are built on a desire to learn, we can try to eliminate the risk of disregarding cultures, but instead bring the richness of diversity into the UK church. My hope is that we can develop a more nuanced theology and understanding of the huge diversity within black-majority traditions, which will in turn better inform our church practices as a whole.

Key principles

1. Regardless of our ethnicity, we are brothers and sisters in Christ.

2. Attitudes matter.

- Humility
- Asking questions
- Listening well
- Wanting to learn
- Avoiding defensiveness

3. The aim of unity is not to supersede diversity; it is to celebrate it. Seeking togetherness by eradicating difference is not a full reflection of the community God has given us.

4. Nothing can replace getting people in the room for face-to-face interaction wherever possible.

5. Use whatever influence you have to provide a platform for the voices of others. Value the position you have, but ensure you are able to empower others through it.

Questions

For personal reflection or discussion in your team

1. How might God be asking you to change as you prepare to respond to this book?

2. How well do you know the culture and the people you are ministering to, as well as those you are trying to reach? Where is there room for growth in your understanding?

3. As a leader, are you willing to adapt your historic ways of doing things, your focus, model of ministry or leadership in order to genuinely demonstrate an integrated expression of church and to reflect the ethnic diversity of the community which surrounds you?

4. How could you use your time to really get to know the individuals within your care, in your church or organisation? How can you better understand their story and cultural background?

5. What platforms could you share with others to empower them and celebrate an element of ethnic diversity that you can't bring on your own?

6. Are there regular opportunities in your church calendar for everyone to get to know others in the community and embrace their cultural expressions?

7. What would a newcomer to your church see in your current practices that would help them to feel welcomed, accepted and invited into the family of God?

Valuing People

How do we value people in a way that crosses cultural boundaries?

YEMI ADEDEJI

My friend Osoba Otaigbe in his book *Building Cultural Intelligence in Church and Ministry* (AuthorHouse, 2016) wrote: "It is a known fact that ministry can take place in a singular cultural environment that is disconnected from other cultural contexts, but in an ever-globalising society such situations are now the exception to the rule."

The challenge with many church leaders and organisations is the lack of competence and the confidence needed to interact with people from other cultures, which may be the result of ignorance, an assumption of cultural superiority, racism or intentional seclusion and separation.

Many BAME communities have experienced a series of personal and systematic acts of discrimination over the years, and such repeated actions have made it difficult not to view any act of unfairness, injustice, prejudice or favouritism through the racial lens. Many white leaders remain largely unaware of their advantage in a society that will require their BAME equivalent to make a double effort before being acknowledged. It is against this background that most leaders hoping to cross cultural barriers must:

- Unlearn to relearn.
- Be aware of cultural blindness.
- Advance from blindness to cultural awareness.
- Be sensitive to other cultures.
- Be competent in cultural intelligence.

My own journey started when I opted out of a thriving black-majority ministry to explore a new path with a white middle-class missionary agency in the UK. This journey was filled with tension and discomfort which brought an interesting change to my life. It was a case of finding myself as a complete alien in a different community and a different context to my original background. It was a change that affected my economic, social and spiritual journey.

What's different?

Attending a conference for the first time in this new context was a rude awakening. I was used to attending conferences in good hotels, wearing a smart suit and supported by clear protocols and a staff team. Instead I found myself staying in a tent in an open field. It was heart-breaking to wake up on the first morning of the conference to find my tent floating after a heavy downpour. That was not the way the black churches ran church conferences. It was a culture shock and a steep learning curve. It was a case of "Get me out of here – I'm black!" Overtime, I have come to understand that different things represent value and importance to different cultures. I submitted myself to adjust my expectations to fit this new context, but also I was conscious that it was never me.

How about arriving hungry as a guest speaker for a church weekend conference, only to be told that a supermarket is across the road to buy my own lunch? It was even more shocking when asked at the end of the conference about my travel mileage, only to be paid to the exact pence per mile as the honorarium. You almost want to ask "Why invite me?" It's interesting to note that the organisers saw nothing wrong with their actions since no one had ever complained or challenged the pattern.

My children always find it funny whenever they are with me when I'm speaking at middle-class Church of England village churches. Despite them having good English accents, it is not uncommon for people to ask them whether they understand English, whether they have just arrived from Africa or when are they going back.

I was once told by a church that it would be better for me to dance for them rather than speak, because the congregation will remember a dancing African missionary. This has become a classic for me, but it came as a shock to be told this while shaking hands with parishioners at the end of their church service. Quite a few people whispered to me about how interesting the service was, but then they added that unfortunately they could not understand me. It baffled me until an old lady made it clear to me. She said: "What passion you show when you shout. I love the demonstration. But that's all I am taking home, because I could not hear nor understand you, except for the few moments when you paused to speak slowly." It became more clear to me when I listened to myself on tape and noticed how fast and loud I could become when excited. It conveys passion but equally can be a turn-off for most Caucasian listeners.

Over time, I have come to understand that if I truly desire to engage as a black Christian and influence white communities, I must learn to engage from a position of humility through service. The truth is I often struggle through discussions and meetings, especially when we have to plan another meeting on the same subject before taking action. I have learnt that process and dialogue are important to the white community; it is so different from the 'one-man leadership', in a dictatorial style, that I was used to.

I have adjusted to take a more flexible approach, learning from every experience and intentionally seeking to see God through the eyes of other cultures, especially those who are marginalised.

I have often wondered how my friend Steve Clifford must have felt in the early years of his appointment as the general director of the Evangelical Alliance when he visited various BAME churches to fellowship with them. I can imagine him being birthed into a new culture of loud music, long services, extravagant dressing, titled office and extended hospitality.

Steve and I both serve as part of the One People Commission at the Evangelical Alliance. We both choose to be intentional about integration despite being ethnically and culturally different. We place a high value on the insight we can both gain by interacting closely with each other and with leaders from other cultures. We choose not to keep our interaction at arm's length, but we work hard to integrate various cultures. This allows the love of Christ to be evident to the community of believers that we both serve and to the wider world.

A cultural interruption

Acts 10 is an amazing story of how Peter is challenged by God to engage and embrace a new narrative that was different from what was normal for him. Cornelius was an officer in the Roman army. A patriotic Jew of that day would naturally dislike or even hate him. As a typical Roman he would have been exposed to the Roman gods such as Jupiter, Augustus, Mars and Venus, although Cornelius was in the category of those the Jews would call God-fearers. The Jewish people of that time respected and appreciated God-fearing Gentiles, but they still wouldn't share their life, homes and food with them.

In preparation for his encounter with Cornelius, God showed Peter a strange vision that contradicted his belief and culture. The vision didn't tell Peter that he would be receiving visitors who were Gentiles, so Peter must have been shocked when he opened his door and saw two servants and a soldier outside. He would have known immediately that they were not Jews, and he would have wondered why God told him to go with them and why God had sent them.

Normally, a Jew would have said something like: "Nice to meet you, but you need to stay out in the street. You can't come inside. If you go down the street a little further, I think you'll probably find a hotel where you can stay." No orthodox Jew would have invited Gentiles into his house. He would not have sat down at the same table with them. He would not have had fellowship with them. It was forbidden.

By entertaining these Gentile guests, Peter went against the customs, culture and traditions of Israel, but not against God's word to embrace a new normal. It is this new normal that God is challenging and calling us to embrace as we embark on a new journey together.

The question to ask is: "Why didn't God make us all the same? What does He want us to learn from each other?" I guess God loves the tapestry of His creation seen in the diverse expression of our differences. Our differences help us to appreciate our multi-faceted amazing God. The uniqueness that we all bring around the table, the differences in culture, expression, clothing, worship, lifestyle, language and food, all help to demonstrate the loving unity and diversity of the Trinity that God wants to reveal to all creation. It's a pointer to the future when what the Apostle John described in Revelation 7:9 becomes a reality: people from every "nation, tribe, people and language" living together in eternity.

Lessons learnt

There are many amazing things that have become my new normal since I've been working with colleagues who are white British. My experience will perhaps mirror that of other people from the BAME community.

As a result of ministering in many white churches, I've come to love their precise timing, structure and brevity, but I haven't allowed that to restrict my flexibility in other contexts. I've also appreciated the servant heart and flexible approach to leadership I see in some Christian communities. I've learnt a lot on how to plan ahead and run every initiative through a thorough, robust process to minimise elements of risk. I love the simple dress code in most white-majority churches, and I have also come to appreciate the value and respect that is placed on each other's gift and calling.

A new normal?

What could a new cultural normal look like for both BAME and white-majority communities? Many leaders, in theory, want diverse people to join their church or organisation, but dig deeper and it seems that nothing is being done intentionally to embrace a new culture. There is a big difference between accepting diversity, becoming inclusive and pursuing integration. Embracing diversity is like inviting people to the party. Inclusion is inviting them to dance. But integration means we host the party together. Embracing diversity can be simply welcoming people to join as long as they accept the majority culture and do not try to bring their culture with them or try to change things. Integration means allowing new people to express their culture in ways that might change the majority culture. In order to be fully integrated we must own up to our fears, insecurities and concerns around what people will think. We must be bold to ask questions that challenge our cultural norm in the way we do things and test the extent of our desire for integration.

Do we have rigid styles?

How rigid is our culture in music, preaching style and fellowship? Are we of the opinion that ethnically diverse people can get involved as long as they like our style (they should not expect us to change for them)? Can we find people of diverse ethnic cultural backgrounds who share in the vision and the mission to move from welcoming diversity through being inclusive to becoming fully integrated?

How prejudiced are we in getting the best person for the job?

It is not uncommon to have ethnically diverse people working in an organisation at a lower level, but it's very rare to find true cultural integration and diversity at leadership level. It's not uncommon that when a leadership position becomes vacant, people only contact and recommend candidates from the network of the people who look like them.

What are our assumed perceptions of ability?

In some churches and conferences, it's okay to invite BAME guests to lead worship or entertain, but they are not considered good enough to speak or preach. I have had to fight a label often attached to me, where I'm part of a leadership team but restricted to leading prayers; I'm hardly ever invited to be the speaker.

What's our style of giving, generous or frugal?

Most BAME churches promote a culture of generosity. Generosity is part of their worship, especially when it concerns individuals who have been a blessing to them. People will want to go the extra mile to welcome, make comfortable, create a warm atmosphere for and, most importantly, be generous to their leaders and visiting ministers. This act of appreciation is not meagre but extravagant because it is seen as an honour not to the person but to them as a representative of God. It's culturally different in some white church contexts. Being frugal and minimal is seen as important because it keeps the leaders humble, with a simple lifestyle. Limiting excesses is seen as evidence of 'good stewardship' in many white ministries.

Exploring non-verbal culture: eye to eye contact

One can judge another person through their lens or their cultural landscape. For example, it is common within an African culture not to look an older person or one's manager or leader in the eyes during conversation. Eye contact is seen as a sign of disrespect, whereas in a white context, a person avoiding eye contact might be considered to be hiding something.

Having conversations

Another non-verbal misunderstanding could be during conversation. In many instances, when talking with people who speak fast, I just smile when I do not understand them. I don't want to embarrass the person by telling them that they are speaking too fast or that I do not understand them. It will be wrong to misinterpret my smile to mean approval of what is being said. Whereas, I find that white British people find it easy to say: "I beg your pardon; I can't hear you. Could you say that again?" I would feel it was rude to ask someone to repeat themselves in this way.

Appearance and dress code

It is not uncommon for white British Christians to dress casually when attending meetings or speaking as a guest minister in most white churches or conferences. It is normal and acceptable, but it is absolutely unacceptable in most BAME church and community contexts. There is an adage that says: "The way you are dressed is the way you will be addressed." It is always important when invited to an event to ask one's host about the dress code. It's possible to appear either overdressed or underdressed, which may appear rude, disrespectful or counter-cultural.

Honour and respect

Honour and respect are valued highly within BAME communities. While it is appropriate to address leaders within a white British context by their first name, it is inappropriate to call an older BAME person by their first name or to address a leader without an appropriate title.

The drive to pursue cultural competence will move us beyond ourselves to a deeper understanding of life from another person's perspective. By cultivating that deeper understanding, we will be drawn closer together and will better reflect the person of Christ.

David Wise

David Wise was sole pastor, then senior pastor, at Greenford Baptist Church from 1987 to 2019. From 2015 to 2019 he served as a part-time interim pastor at various London Baptist churches, and a part-time tutor at Formission College. He is now the programme leader for the Masters in Spiritual Formation at Waverley Abbey College and is part way through a DTh programme focussing on the creation of genuine multi-ethnic church communities. David is white British.

When I came to Greenford Baptist in October 1987, the congregation was almost entirely white British. Despite being in a multicultural context outside the building, fewer than 10 people in the congregation were black; from its congregation to its worship style, the church was white.

We'd always wanted anyone and everyone to feel really welcome, becoming a community where people quickly found a home, a family and a place where they belonged. Sadly, however, I discovered that our neighbours were on the receiving end of racial prejudice in the community around our church building. For example, on the evening that a Dominican family moved onto a street near the church, they had all their windows smashed by people saying they didn't want black people in the community. What I found even more distressing was hearing that people had also experienced racial prejudice from within our own church.

In response, I called a meeting of our leadership team and asked a couple of our recent black converts to share their experience of living in the community and being part of the church. It was a very painful evening, but it brought about a much-needed openness to change. As a church, we committed to continually confront and challenge racial prejudice, and it marked a huge step towards becoming a multi-ethnic church. More than just challenging damaging behaviour, we wanted to celebrate the cultures within our church. We longed to be fully integrated in the way that we prayed, worshipped, did social events etc., not tokenistically, but wholeheartedly.

In 2015, when my regular involvement with the church came to an end, we had 47 different nationalities represented and many more ethnicities. We would sing in a wide range of different languages and styles. For example, when singing in Hindi, we would do call and response, use a tabla drum, bells, and sit on the floor. In prayer, people could pray in English or their own first language, and we found that God brought a great freedom with this. In preaching, we'd encourage the speaker to use their own style, drawing on illustrations from their own culture.

I discovered early on that I couldn't tell people what to do; I had to embody those principles myself. People were encouraged to see this in me and I'm so glad that they've come along with me on the journey. Many times, God spoke to me about the changes that needed to happen and I knew they had to start in my own life, which led me to do things like learn Portuguese. This communicated to people in the church that English was not seen as God's language and that I was willing to struggle, learn, and change.

I also recognised that I personally used a white British interpretation of the scriptures. In response to this realisation, I did a Masters in Biblical Interpretation so that I could further appreciate how our cultural identity and context determines what we read into any given passage. We developed a way of handling the Bible on a Sunday morning: where I would ask lots of questions (and listen to the answers!) to help people draw from their own backgrounds and bring together a rich, shared interpretation of scripture.

Early on, I developed a metaphor for Greenford Baptist Church of the church being a tapestry. The thing about a tapestry is that it is the distinctiveness of the different threads that makes the picture so beautiful. I hear the term 'melting pot' about multicultural church, where everything is mixed together, but a tapestry is different. There is no quick way to make a tapestry or an integrated church, but we want to keep the distinctive colours and threads that God has brought into our community, and work together to reflect the beauty of His unity amongst diversity.

Ann Clifford

Ann Clifford is a member of her local church leadership team, a speaker, devoted Street Pastor, magazine and book contributor, playwright, screenwriter and author of *Time to Live: The Beginner's Guide to Saying Goodbye* and *Where is God in our 21st Century World?* She is white British and has been committed for more than 10 years to working with Steve Clifford towards greater diversity, unity and integration in the Evangelical Alliance.

In the UK lots of us find ourselves living amongst wonderfully diverse cultures. So many of the people I meet are Christians who bring a dynamic, Holy Spirit-filled, evangelical expectation and energy to bless this country. Culture boundaries are not just about the things we can see. It's not just about the national dish, the fashions we wear, or even the places we live. A large amount of what we do, say, think, believe and, to some extent, feel is shaped by the culture we grew up in. How do we value all forms of diversity? Can we open ourselves to change and work together so that Jesus may realise His investment and we may glorify God together?

Mother Theresa said: "Every time you smile at someone, it is an action of love, a gift to that person, a beautiful thing."

Steve and I have opened our home to Christian leaders for years, rejoicing in the rich diversity to be found in the kingdom of God. Our longing is for people to find each other, for barriers to be broken down, and for deep relationships to be forged. There is only one rule, which we made after our first garden party: always have someone available to answer the door. There was so much noise the first time, that an honoured guest failed to gain entrance and left, eating the chocolates he had brought on his return home.

After a great deal of discussion between us, Steve and I began an annual garden party on a Monday afternoon, the day off for most leaders. It meant the event could be alcohol free, which would suit many; and who doesn't like cake with scones and cream thrown in for good measure? Although, I had to learn to adjust the food to accommodate different dietary requirements.

My main regret is that I did not educate myself more before welcoming such diversity. Now I read books and take every opportunity to gain first-hand experience with different groupings. I want to include my adult children and grandchildren in all I discover. What have I learnt?

First and foremost, I've learnt to love people; so many mistakes can be overcome with the love of Jesus. Also, be yourself and allow people to know you. People find each other one meal at a time. Eating together, particularly if you open your home, incorporates acceptance, respect and honour, so extend hospitality. It is important to help people to feel safe. Don't make assumptions and keep an open mind, avoiding your own stereotypes. Remember, one person does not represent an entire ethnic group. I was shocked and saddened to learn that many of our guests had not been invited into a white person's home before. Uncharted territory makes us all nervous and none of us want to "do the wrong thing". Be honest about your own bias. Whatever our culture, we all have to battle with racism; it is insidious, and we have grown up with it all around us. And finally, I've learnt to give, give and give again.

Key principles

1. This will be a long journey and may take many years. Don't set out if you have not considered the cost and are not willing to pay it personally.

2. Cultures other than our own can teach us valuable lessons.

3. Be willing to learn – go and see what the other person is doing, to observe and make a point of extending the hand of friendship. Give time, make time; sharing a stage is not enough.

4. Allow yourself to be known in order to build relationship. Trust takes a great deal of time to build. Be a friend.

5. Much of what you believe will need to be questioned. The truth of God is the same, but how you express it might need to be better culturally informed.

Questions

For personal reflection or discussion in your team

1. Why do you want to work towards increased ethnic integration? What is your personal motivation?

2. What does your vision for unity look like? Who is included in this vision and what are the steps you can outline together to realise it?

3. What is the next step God is calling you to take on the journey towards ethnic integration in your context?

4. What cultural changes and challenges are you afraid of? How can they be overcome?

5. How can you extend hospitality and increase your understanding of how people from other ethnicities view life, purpose and faith?

Communicating Effectively

How do we need to change our attitudes and means of communication to better engage with others?

STEVE CLIFFORD

In Israel Olofinjana's book *Turning the Tables on Mission* (Instant Apostle, 2013), Jose Carlos Lara, a Brazilian missionary in Northern Ireland, tells the painful story of establishing an outreach which taught English lessons for foreign mothers based at a local church. The initial problem involved the church volunteers threatening to boycott the creche if they kept bringing black children to their creche. This issue was solved by moving the day of the classes and recruiting new volunteers. But the situation escalated.

"Every week we provided some refreshments for the children and mothers – simple things such as tea and coffee for adults and squash with biscuits for the children. A few days after the problem with the church volunteers, we were surprised to find that their beakers were locked in a cupboard in the church kitchen. Initially we thought there had been a misunderstanding and that they had been locked away by mistake, but when Keith went to talk to the person in charge, she replied that they did not want to share the beakers with black children, fearing contamination. That was one of the worst days of our ministry there. How could a person who called herself a Christian be so racist?" (P85-86, *Turning the Tables on Mission,* Israel Olofinjana, Joel Edwards and Ram Gidoomal, Instant Apostle, 2013)

I don't believe these Christians would have viewed themselves as racist, but they had presuppositions based on ignorance, which determined their behaviour. Their behaviour had not been redeemed by the work of the cross; it was racist. As we have embarked on this journey of discovery over the last few years, it has been important to recognise my own blind spots and behavioural patterns, that needed to be challenged and adjusted. We can all live with presuppositions and stereotypes that influence our views of each other.

The impact of the Fall

The first chapters of Genesis paint a picture of the impact of man's decision to turn away from God (the Fall). In Genesis 11, this comes to a head with a strange story of a tower being built. We are told those building the tower were motivated by the ambition to make a name for themselves and to avoid being scattered. The construction project is aided by the fact that the whole world shared the same language. God's response was to create confusion, thus stopping the building, scattering the people, and making sure they could not communicate. In Genesis 12, we get the first insight into God's intention. He is instigating a rescue plan. It started with a man, Abraham; it expanded to a family, a clan, a tribe, a nation, but did not find its fullness until a Saviour, the Messiah, was sent and a new community of God's people was established. The day of Pentecost, the birthday of the church, sees the curse of Babel overturned as the Holy Spirit enabled people to understand Jesus' followers who were speaking different languages. God sends out a powerful signal that the rescue plan, which was promised to Abraham, was being fulfilled and the whole of humanity, every tribe and nation, was going to hear what happened through the work of Jesus the saviour.

The book of Acts tells the story of how this message ripples out from Jerusalem, through Judea and Samaria to the ends of the Earth (Acts 1:8), and how the emerging church begins to reflect the ethnic diversity that had always been God's plan. The journey wasn't smooth; there was deep-seated ignorance and prejudices which needed to be overcome if this community was to be a family, regardless of their gender, religion, social status, or ethnic background. This journey continues to this day in local churches and national ministries, and is either advanced or hindered as we take steps to communicate with each other.

What has this meant for the Evangelical Alliance and what could it mean for you?

The Evangelical Alliance's response to the challenge of scripture did not begin in 2010. Thank God for those who had gone before, including Philip Mohabir, the great pioneering missionary from Guyana. He arrived in the UK in 1956 and, in the 1980s, started the African and Caribbean Evangelical Alliance (ACEA). Rev Katei Kirby joined ACEA as a trustee in 2002 and was appointed as CEO in 2005. And of course, my friend and predecessor as general director, Joel Edwards, who began his work with the Evangelical Alliance as leader of the ACEA. However, as we have outlined in chapter 1, back in 2010, it did seem as if God was asking us to go both deeper and wider in our response to His call for unity. If we were serious in answering the question "How does the Evangelical Alliance need to change in order to reflect, represent and serve the diversity of the evangelical community across the UK?" every area of our work had to be open to challenge:

- The diversity of our staff team
- The makeup of our council, board and various advisory groups and commissions
- The Evangelical Alliance's public profile: our publications, websites and social media
- The agenda of the Evangelical Alliance: the issues were we speaking about

Alongside these more structural challenges, there were a multitude of further lessons to learn, many of which are picked up below or in the 'Lessons from the Journey' summary at the end of the book.

11 key lessons learnt

1. It's complex

While inward migration to the UK has been part of our history for thousands of years, and our country is increasingly recognising its multiracial makeup, many of our Evangelical Alliance members live in communities that are relatively mono-ethnic in makeup. However, the experience in the story at the beginning of this chapter means we all need to embrace the racial diversity of the church here in the UK, celebrating that diversity and learning how we can best relate to each other in the complexity of our cultural differences. For some of us, a better understanding of the experience of BAME Christians will involve us being willing to do some work in asking people to tell their personal stories or perhaps some further research.

- Churches across the UK come in a wide mixture of ethnic expressions. These include:
  - white British – host community dominant with possibly a few from other ethnic backgrounds with a white leader.
  - BAME churches – with one dominant ethnicity, but possibly a few from other backgrounds, and with a leader from the dominant ethnicity. Some of these churches will have services conducted in languages other than English.
  - BAME churches, but with a number of ethnic backgrounds within it – with possibly a white or BAME leader.
  - Historically white background church that has widened its ethnic mix – could have either a white or BAME leader.

It's easy to assume that people from all ethnic minority backgrounds will think or act in the same way. There are of course a wide range of views, personalities and ways of doing church, both between ethnicities and among those of the same ethnicity. Some of the greatest varieties of church expressions and models of ministries are found within ethnic minority churches.

Things change the longer an ethnic minority group has settled in the country. First-generation migrants (those born outside the UK) will differ enormously from second, third and fourth generation migrants who were born and educated in the UK and have made the UK their permanent home (see chapter 8).

Some parts of our cities have experienced what has been called 'white flight' when an increasing number of BAME people have moved into an area and the indigenous white population has moved out, because of the changing culture of their community. Sadly, some churches have experienced a similar dynamic as the historically white and perhaps older congregation has struggled to embrace the changes associated with a more ethnically mixed congregation and perhaps a non-white church leader. While such stories are deeply disappointing, thankfully there are also numerous stories where change has been embraced, and both the white and ethnic minority members of the church have been enriched.

2. Language is important

For some time, I used to refer to 'migrant churches' until it was pointed out that many within ethnic minority churches were not migrants; in fact, they had been born and brought up in the UK. They are fully British and not here temporarily. Often people are referred to as 'those of colour', but that suggests that 'white' is not a colour but is the norm.

In one of our publications, we referred to 'the English population', hoping this would be seen to refer to all those of all ethnicities who were living in England. We were, however, informed that for many, when they see the word 'English' they assume you are talking about white English people. Of course, we can use BME (black and minority ethnic) or BAME (black, Asian and minority ethnic). All language or abbreviations carry some potential problems and can feel somewhat clinical. We increasingly refer to ethnic minority churches or the ethnic minority community, alongside 'BAME' churches and communities, as you'll see throughout this resource, but we realise that for churches in city contexts like London, Christians from a BAME background are actually in the majority.

3. Subtle racism

While some racism is blatant, other racism is more subtle and more difficult to detect. Let me give you a few examples to see if they resonate:

- Pigeonholing ethnic minority leaders on subjects they can speak about or assuming their best contribution to a meeting will always be to pray.
- Humour which focuses on the same subjects such as differences in timekeeping, organisation or approach to finances, without taking the opportunity to explore our different priorities and approaches.
- Dismissing the experiences of ethnic minority Christians when they are shared. George Yancy commented from a US context that, subtle racism is particularly hard for African Americans who have faced personal or systemic acts of discrimination throughout their lifetimes. Such "repeated encounters have made it difficult for them to avoid viewing any act of unfairness, injustice or insensitivity through a racial grid". When such encounters are dismissed as being open to other interpretations or over-sensitive, the individual is again left feeling that they are not respected or heard.
- Making negative comments about others when they aren't in the room is always problematic, whatever the issue being discussed.
- Some white Christians have proudly announced that they are 'colour blind' as if that is a virtue. Ben Lindsay points out that, "If white church members do not have a degree of colour consciousness, they will ignore the realities, concerns, joys and fears of colour experience" (*We Need to Talk About Race*, Ben Lindsay. SPCK Publishing, 2019). The unity we aspire to is not one of uniformity, but unity in the midst of our diversity. It is a unity that does not deny our differences, but looks to celebrate and enjoy them. I'm aware of so many local churches that are now exploring this kind of celebration:
  - Church parties with a vast array of food from around the world.
  - Public prayer in the heart language of the individual rather than having to be in English.
  - Worship with a variety of styles that reflect the different cultures in the church.
  - Flags displayed from all the nations represented in the church.
- Structures are allowed to exist that exclude BAME individuals from the decision-making process.

4. Titles matter

Titles can be a minefield. Rev Rodrigo Assis daSilva describes his arrival at Emmanuel Baptist Church, a multicultural church in Thamesmead: "As I arrived in Thamesmead, I had to give my real name 'Rodigo' with a strong 'R' at the beginning that sounds like an 'H' as almost no one could pronounce it properly. The majority of white people in the church simply called me by what became my first name – 'Rob'. The majority of older black African and Caribbean folk would call me, 'Pastor', 'Sir' or even 'Reverend'. However, the black African and Caribbean young people tended to call me by my first name and were often rebuked or told off by the older black folk who would label the youngsters as being disrespectful to the pastor." (*Turning the Tables on Mission*, edited by Israel Olofinjana. Instant Apostle, 2013)

As a white church leader relating to the BAME churches, I thought it was important to respect the titles within the churches I was relating to. Initially, both publicly and privately, I would preface the person's name with the title, Pastor/Bishop/Reverend/Doctor/Apostle/Overseer. Often, I would be encouraged to drop the title privately, but I would always use the title publicly, and particularly as I got up to speak I would express appreciation to the senior leader or leaders who were in the room, using their preferred title.

5. Honouring

As I built relationships with many ethnic minority leaders and visited their churches, I realised that in most, honouring leaders was very important. I received such honour myself as they welcomed me and realised that it was vital that I respected this biblical and cultural expression.

What might this look like?

- Use the preferred title in both public and private communications.
- Meet visiting speakers at the door and escort them to an appropriate place to prepare for the meeting.
- Express appreciation and welcome before a guest is invited to speak. A visiting leader should, wherever possible, be given some opportunity to participate in the meeting, if only briefly, or at the very least be acknowledged during the meeting.
- Food and hospitality are very important in many ethnic minority churches. I am regularly sent home with a large basket of goodies following a visit to a church, and many times I will be invited to stay to eat a hot meal.
- Certain events are very important in the life of the ethnic minority churches, such as annual festivals, celebrations, conferences, assemblies and funerals. I've made it a discipline to visit as

many as I can. They provide an amazing insight into what God is doing in the community and it's also an opportunity to build relationships.

- Smart appearance for functions, church meetings and private gatherings is a sign of respect.
- Attitudes to alcohol vary greatly across the church worldwide. Within most ethnic minority churches, alcohol would not be socially acceptable and indeed a leader seen drinking alcohol could cause offence.
- In many African and Caribbean churches, it would be expected that the pastor would drive a relatively new, smart car. The congregation would feel a degree of embarrassment if they weren't. This attitude to cars would not be true in most predominately white churches; in fact, too smart a car could be problematic. This can create an interesting problem. Yemi usually drives around in an impressive BMW; I drive a 12-year-old Volkswagen Golf. I understand from Yemi, when travelling to speak at a white church, he has been known to park around the corner from the church so as not to raise questions about his car. I have the same experience when visiting a BAME church: I confess, I do feel a little embarrassed by my old car sitting beside the pastor's car in the car park.

6. Generosity

Generosity is another value of many ethnic minority churches. During my time as general director, the Evangelical Alliance has received some of the most generous gifts for speaking that I've ever received in all my years of public ministry. As we relate to the ethnic minority churches, it is important that, as best we are able, we find ways to respect and reciprocate that generosity.

7. Women in leadership and ministry

As within the white British church, approaches to women in leadership and ministry will vary within the ethnic minority churches. While some have fully embraced women in leadership roles, and indeed there are some high-profile women leading ministries, many BAME churches remain both in practice and theology unconvinced. I've visited many churches where head covering is a norm for women, and I understand a small number of churches would separate men and women.

For some BAME churches this issue is being discussed. I recently attended a national leadership assembly of a large BAME denomination where these issues were vigorously debated and where the denomination explored the possibility of changing its historic practice.

8. Prayer

When Dr Tani Omideyi became chair of the Evangelical Alliance board in 2016, he insisted that we changed the way that we met. The business agenda, circulated prior to the meeting, was carefully designed with periods of time given over to prayer and listening to God and anything He would wish to say to us on the agenda items just covered. This approach refreshed our meetings. When meeting with ethnic minority leaders, whether privately or in public settings, expect prayer to be part of that meeting. This style of meeting has now become part of the culture within the Evangelical Alliance and 'prayerful' has become one of our four core values. I'm convinced one of the great gifts BAME churches have brought to the UK church over recent years has been focused and passionate prayer. Local churches all over the UK are benefitting from that investment, as prayer has become a priority and the heart of many churches.

9. Making contact

Understanding how we best communicate with each other is vital and can be a source of some frustration. Within the BAME churches, often face-to-face meetings are welcomed and well-received. It is, however, important to remember that many pastors and leaders are bi-vocational, so meetings during the working day can be difficult. This fact also impacts on some of the ethnic minority leaders being able to attend daytime leaders' gatherings.

- Once face-to-face meetings have taken place, phone calls are likely to be more successful than an email. In fact, almost anything can be better than any email. WhatsApp or texts are also useful if you know the person well.
- RSVPs provide an interesting point of cultural interchange. For myself, if I indicate I'm planning to attend an event, it means it's in my diary and, short of a major crisis, I will be there. Should such a crisis occur, I'd feel duty bound to give a full explanation. Within some cultures, an RSVP response indicates a statement of intent at that time. It means "It's possible I will come" or "I currently plan to be there, however things could change and if I do come, I may well bring somebody else as well."

10. Actions speak louder than words

In producing a resource such as this, there is a danger that we can create an impression that ethnic unity is a difficult thing and we reinforce an 'us and them' approach to the life of the church locally and nationally. I thank God that as I look across the church in the UK, I see significant progress has been made in breaking down barriers and building bridges between the diverse expressions of the evangelical church. I am thankful to God for the contribution the Evangelical Alliance has made, particularly through the work of the One People Commission. While words are important, we all know that actions speak louder than words. It's our body language that shouts the loudest. It is important that people see the diverse ethnic expressions of the church working together locally and nationally, sharing platforms, speaking up on issues that are important, sitting around talking together, making decisions, and publicly affirming each other. In many localities, this is expressed through:

- Shared buildings
- Exchange of pulpits
- Public prayer and evangelistic events
- Social action projects

11. Conflict

Any family will at some stage face conflict; in fact, it's not always wrong. If handled well it can be productive. Over the years, the Evangelical Alliance has had to face its own share of conflict. A historic document entitled 'Our Relational Commitments' dates back to 1846 and stands beside the Evangelical Alliance 'Basis of Faith'. It has provided a great framework for handling disagreement well.

However, based upon what you have already read, we should not be surprised if conflict is faced in the area of our relationships across diverse ethnic expressions. I look back now with some pain on two or three meetings when we did not conduct ourselves well. Strong opinions were expressed. Nothing of itself is wrong with that, but language was used which wasn't always handled with care, and it was interpreted as a personal attack. On one occasion, I didn't close the discussion down quickly enough and, when an apology was made, not everyone was in the room. As I look back now, I realise just how painful this was for those involved, but also how easily this could have derailed all we had been working towards. I am convinced that while we hadn't handled things as well as we should have, we were also facing a spiritual attack. When our unity is a means of showing the world what God is like, spiritual attacks should not surprise us.

The issue of venues to worship in has become a major difficulty for ethnic minority churches across the UK. Our publication *Firm Foundations: helping churches find places to call home* was published in 2018 to address the issues associated with church property. While sharing buildings with other churches has been a source of rich blessing, it has also at times resulted in significant conflict, particularly when there has been a mismatch of expectations. (*Firm Foundations* provides a checklist for such arrangements.)

Of course, different cultures approach disagreement in different ways:

- White British people have a tendency towards avoidance, 'shoving it under the carpet' pretending it's not happening, hoping it will go away.
- Among some Africans, even the most insignificant disagreement will result in raised voices in such a way that it can feel that war is about to break out.
- Within certain Asian cultures, there's such a reluctance to cause offence that no expression of disappointment or disagreement will be communicated.

Lessons learnt in the midst of conflict:

- Love each other and believe the best of each other.
- Take care with words, being slow to speak and determined to listen.
- Ask questions and be slow to make statements.
- Avoid defensiveness.
- Be quick to forgive, but don't avoid the issue.
- Look beyond the words to the attitude of heart.
- Different cultures disagree in different ways. It's helpful to understand these differences and to respond appropriately.

Roy Crowne

Roy Crowne is executive director of HOPE Together, a mission initiative bringing the UK church together to make Jesus known with words and actions. His passion is to see the church working together for the purpose of mission. Prior to leading HOPE, Roy worked for Youth for Christ for 28 years, the last 13 years as national director. Roy is convinced that no one person or situation is beyond hope. Born in London's East End, he is white British. His close friendships with Yemi Adedeji and Ade Omooba, both part of the HOPE leadership team, and Pastor Osh of the Chinese Church, have challenged him to seek increased diversity and to broaden his vision of the gospel in Christ.

I've discovered that it's quite often the things I don't say that speak far louder than the things I do. In reality, the messages that are sent subliminally by our leadership teams, communities and processes can communicate much more about our values than the vision we think we're promoting.

For me, this came out predominantly through the Theos report that we commissioned for Hope 08. Steve Clifford was the chair of HOPE at the time, and the overriding lesson from the report was that we didn't engage enough with people from diverse ethnicities and backgrounds. With Steve at the helm, we took this very seriously and decided that we had to do something about it.

We knew that we had to be in the room with people in order to communicate better, so the first step was for Laurence Singlehurst and myself to meet with a group of BAME church leaders and listen to how they felt. We heard much about their pain from how the white constituency had treated them, often excluding them or side-lining them from the church – whether intentionally or not. As a result of that pivotal conversation, we made the decision to bring in someone who could consistently provide the voice and perspective that we were desperately missing from our leadership. This was when we appointed Yemi Adedeji as assistant director of HOPE.

What followed from 2010 to 2012 was a very significant journey of re-evaluating how we functioned as an organisation, and what message we were sending. We had to recognise our own prejudices and preconceptions, and laugh at some of the things we were doing and how they could be perceived. We committed to investing in relationships, and being prepared to have two-way communication. And we had to be prepared for the relationships we were making and the conversations we were having to lead to genuine change, rather than just ticking boxes for good publicity.

If we were genuinely going to communicate God's heart for diversity then we needed to ensure none of the changes we were making were purely tokenism. At every point, we had to see communication as two-way – to listen as much as we talked – and we had to keep remembering that we communicate through our processes and behaviour as much as we do through our values and what we say.

Ultimately, this made us aware of a whole range of areas where we had been subconsciously excluding people from non-white backgrounds. For example, the white-majority church is renowned for loving processes and procedures. The black-majority church, however, often makes a decision and then just gets on with it! By valuing our processes and procedures too highly, we'd given the impression that we didn't value the input or involvement of people from non-white backgrounds.

Similarly, in my town there was a lady from the Redeemed Christian Church of God who originated from Nigeria. She was never at the church leaders' mid-week breakfast. I approached her and asked why she didn't attend, and she responded that it was because she worked full-time alongside being a pastor, so couldn't get there for a weekday, an immediate barrier for her. Also, she said that her passionate and loud style of praying would not be appreciated, and when she had attended no one talked to her. I encouraged her to come along and to be herself when she prayed. On one occasion she was able to share a fantastic devotion that totally changed white perceptions of people from BAME churches. Sadly, even after her wonderful contribution that morning, the other leaders weren't willing to move the meeting and so the message remained that we weren't prepared to make changes so that she could be included.

It is moments like this that have simply served to fuel the fire for me at HOPE Together over the years, ensuring that we rectified the message that we were communicating. Rather than continuing to perpetuate a message that says people from non-white backgrounds aren't welcome, we want to continue to honour and make space at the table for all of God's people.

Key principles

1. Ask God to reveal blind spots, ignorance, even racism, which is affecting attitudes and behaviour.

2. Be prepared to listen before you lead. Communication is as much about learning and understanding others as it is about expressing what we think.

3. Take care with language. Recognise the limitations on any words used.

4. Remember that titles matter.

5. Learn how to honour well.

6. Practise generosity as a key value.

7. Learn the best way to make contact and to stay in touch.

8. Take care when conflict occurs. The issue could be spiritual as well as practical.

1. What is the key message you want to send to people from different backgrounds in your community?

2. What are the presuppositions you live with, of those who are ethnically different from yourself? Is there any hint of superiority in your attitudes? Could they possibly damage your relationships and provide an inroad to racism?

3. How might you need to change your approach to communication in order to reach out beyond the comfort of your own ethnicity?

4. What messages might you be subliminally sending through your current structure and processes?

5. Who are the people who can regularly provide honest feedback on the way that you and your church are perceived?

6. Does the biblical teaching in your church consistently explore the themes of unity and your relationships across all ethnic backgrounds, while at the same time challenging both ethnic minority and white British Christians as to the unbiblical aspects of their culture?

4

Leadership and Teambuilding

How does our leadership need to change to embrace a new landscape?

YEMI ADEDEJI

In the last 25 years, I have been privileged to serve both as a leader, or part of the leadership team, of various settings ranging from business, church, charity and corporate organisations.

My experiences range from serving as the main leader in a majority African or BAME context of a church, and in some instances as the leader in a mixed church community. In a few circumstances I have also served as the only black person in a leadership position in an all-white context. My engagement in each context is different, based on the cultural intelligence and expectations of the group.

Leadership in a black ethnic setting

Leading in an all-black context in my early days as a church leader was never a problem. People in this context looked forward to hearing the vision and directives from the leadership. Commitment from followers was robust where the leadership was clear about its dream and purpose. It was never a duty of a committee to make a decision; it's the duty of the leader to lead with intent from the top.

I remember having a team meeting with my leaders and asking for suggestions on the way forward. It was a big mistake at several different levels. Those who wanted to be heard dominated the conversation and made strong cases. In retrospect, I can see that this weakened my role as a leader, as I might have been perceived as being weak. At the other level, those who remained quiet were unanimous in their challenge to me. They were wondering why I was asking for direction from other people, if I was indeed called by God to lead, and whether I was actually qualified to be their leader. According to them, my job was to hear from God, and tell them what to do.

The danger in this leadership style is the abuse of authority and the leadership position, which can lead to control, dictatorship and oppression.

Leadership in a mixed ethnic setting

As I have progressed in leadership over the years, I have also found myself leading in a mixed team. A mixed team is both complex and inspirational. It requires a high level of emotional intelligence and cultural awareness. An individual's background shapes their worldview, behaviour and reaction to the simplest issue of concern. Leading a mixed team requires humility and self-consciousness if the intention is to have the contribution and participation of everyone. It's a case of 'one cap doesn't fit all' but, where interaction and cooperation has been well coordinated, it has always produced an exciting result.

Leading as director of the One People Commission at the Evangelical Alliance has helped me to develop a new narrative for mixed leadership. We currently have church leaders from Europe, Asia, Africa, and North and South America in this group. The majority of the leaders come from the black and minority ethnic communities. It's interesting to note that different methods of communication, engagement and conversation styles have to be adopted to suit an individual's background, ethnicity and culture.

For example, when planning for a meeting, just sending an email alone will get the white British leaders' attention, but it will have to be a relational communication in order to get the black and the minority ethnic groups into the room. When preparing for a collaborative initiative, it is paramount to get the minority group in the loop from the onset rather than asking them to join when all the plans have been made.

In recent years, I have been asked to advise a global UK charity serving people in Africa. In my consultation with their leadership team, it was obvious that they need to change and to be open to understand, embrace and intentionally increase staff, leadership team and board members to reflect the people they have been called to serve.

Leadership in a white ethnic setting

Many years ago I was co-opted as the only black trustee and director of one of the oldest and largest UK mission agencies. Initially I was elated, but I soon came to feel that my appointment was a token to portray inclusion, not to contribute from my knowledge. The most significant contribution I was allowed to make was to pray either to open or close the meetings. It was a difficult time as I struggled to understand the all-white middle-class British folks. They talked to each other and literally ignored my presence in the room. Whenever I chose to make a point, everyone stopped, listened to me as if I was stupid, then continued without ever making mention of my contribution. I was forced to raise my voice in a few instances because I was being ignored and disregarded. The response was to be told to speak slowly because I apparently have an accent and to lower my voice because I was shouting and making others feel uncomfortable. I've found it to be a big challenge to lead as a BAME leader in all-white context.

There are other instances where it has been difficult to understand the actual meaning of an indirect but polite response in a white British culture. In my experience, here are some examples of what a white British person might say and what they actually mean:

- "I hear what you say" might mean "I disagree and I do not wish to discuss any further."
- "With the greatest respect..." might mean "I think you are a fool."
- "Not bad" might mean "good" or "very good".
- "Quite good" might mean "a bit disappointing".
- "Perhaps you would like to think about it" might mean "This is an order. Do it or be prepared to justify yourself."
- "Very interesting" might mean "I do not agree."
- "Could we consider the options?" might mean "I do not like your idea."
- "I will bear it in mind" might mean "I will do nothing about it."

- "Perhaps you could give that some more thought" might mean "It is a bad idea; don't do it."
- "I'm sure it's my fault" might mean "It's actually your fault."
- "This is a brave option to consider" might mean "You must be crazy."
- "You must come for dinner sometime" might mean "This not an invitation; I'm just being polite."
- "Not entirely helpful" might mean "Completely useless".

My friend Roy Crowne could tell multiple stories of his own experience as a white person working with BAME churches in the UK. Here is one. Roy says: "One thing I have discovered, which still remains a puzzle to me as I work together with leaders from BAME churches was that we had a different clock; a different interpretation of timing. I learnt that there was western time, and there was African and Caribbean time. This was highlighted to me as I started to visit many of the BAME churches. I was once going to speak at one of their churches; the starting time was 10:30am according to the invitation. On arrival I discovered there were only a few of us there; it was only after an hour that most people arrived. The worship kept on going to the point that I was beginning to wonder what time we would actually leave. The service went on 2½ hours on that occasion, and compared with my culture, it was a completely different style of worship and liturgy. It was fascinating talking to the pastor afterwards on how to embrace their host community. I suggested that in order for his church to integrate and work with the leaders of the host community, some things would need to change to recognise the cultural differences; adjustments would be needed to serve the host community."

I've always wondered whether the folks in the Bible had the same challenges we face today in multi-ethnic leadership working together as a team. Then it became obvious that nothing is new, as detailed in Luke's writing of the Acts of the Apostles.

Multi-ethnic leadership and scripture

"Now in the church (assembly) at Antioch there were prophets (inspired interpreters of the will and purposes of God) and teachers: Barnabas, Symeon who was called Niger [Black], Lucius of Cyrene, Manaen a member of the court of Herod the tetrarch, and Saul" (Acts 13:1 AMPC).

The Bible gave five names of people in the leadership sphere of the church, namely:

- Barnabas: A Jew originally from Cyprus
- Symeon: (Niger) A black African
- Lucius: From Cyrene, Libya in North Africa
- Manaen: A foster kid brought up by the wicked Antipas and a member of the court of Herod the tetrarch but serving as youth pastor
- Saul: From Turkey as we know it today

Diverse leadership team

What was evident in this church was a diverse pastoral team that represented the dynamics of its local community. It was a local church in a global world. It was a church of multi-racial leadership, pluralistic leadership and complimentary leadership with a balanced and diverse gifting.

The success of the first multi-ethnic church in the Bible was as a result of its intentional multi-ethnic leadership. Up until the time that the believers came over from Cyprus and Cyrene in Africa. The church in Antioch was mono-ethnic, ministering only to the Jews, which restricted its growth and influence. The explosion of the Antioch church was as a result of the diverse ethnic background of its leadership.

The leaders of the church in Antioch were faced with a challenge similar to what many leaders hoping to influence a multi-racial community would have been facing today.

The city of Antioch in its day was the third largest city of the Roman Empire. It was equivalent to London in the UK, Paris in France, or New York in the USA. It was a cosmopolitan city of wealth, commerce and tourism. The population living in Antioch in those days was a mix of migrants from across the world: Jews, Greeks, Romans, Persians, Indians, Chinese and Africans; very similar to any cosmopolitan city anywhere in the world today. It was a sinful city full of immorality, prostitution, idolatry and superstition. It is against this background that the first multi-ethnic church leadership was birthed. Their diverse leadership team reflected the host community and as a result they were well equipped to welcome, influence and serve their community.

A guide for multi-ethnic leadership

Bottom-up versus top-down leadership

There is a sharp difference in cultural expressions of leadership. Most white British leadership seem to operate a bottom-up, collective leadership style, which can be frustrating and challenging to most BAME communities that see leadership as a call and assignment to an individual or a team. BAME churches are used to a strong, passionate, charismatic leadership style that will guide and inspire the followers. Not long ago I was leading a seminar on ethnic diversity and leadership at the Gather Summit – a unity movement conference. The participants were spread across diverse ethnicities. There were also equally different views on how each participant saw leadership and hierarchy. Most white British leaders are against hierarchy and top-down leadership and thus advocate for equality across the board. This is alien and strange to most BAME leaders whose cultural experience, exposure and background has been shaped by hierarchy and directive from the leader at the top. This may create tension within a group with a diverse ethnic mix. It is therefore important to listen and respect each other's position and to be flexible, adjusting where possible.

There is a school of thought that the emerging generation in BAME communities dislike hierarchy and top-down leadership. This might be true in some cases, but it is also true that the emerging generation aspire to be mentored, led and given direction without being ordered or disrespected.

Appointment by calling versus appointment by qualification

Appointments into key leadership positions in most BAME constituencies are made by acknowledging God's call and recognising evidence of the assignment on an individual that is confirmed by two or more people. This might be followed by a simple process that is often rooted in joint affirmation from the other leaders. It's always a case of appointing the person with the call as opposed to the person with the right qualifications, a pedigree that might have performed well at the interview.

Long-term planning versus impulsive action

The western culture seems to prefer a structured long-term plan for initiatives, projects and vision. This can often seem rigid to BAME communities who are impulsive and flexible with plans, initiatives and delivery, to the point of changing direction at any time without a long process of consultation. Most BAME leaders operate as entrepreneurs when making decisions, while most white British leaders go through processes likened to the civil service.

Governance by process versus governance by outcome

The western culture tends to place value on written documents, contracts and policies in contrast to the BAME culture where unwritten social dynamics take priority; outcome is more meaningful than the process. White leaders may benefit from learning how to step back from the logic-based approach in which they have been trained, and acknowledging the more spontaneous insights of the BAME leaders. The position and understanding of the Charity Commission, in some cases, has helped shape governance and accountability in accordance with the prevailing law of the land around finance, while safeguarding and other policies have helped to shape the interaction of the BAME leaders and their new communities.

Leading with healthy hope versus leading with healthy caution

Most BAME leaders don't need to have the resources to hand before embarking on an audacious project. They are driven by faith and the believe that failure is better than doing nothing. Most white British leaders will initiate action only when the resources are available and with little or no room for risk or reputational damage. This can often create frustration when trying to reach joint decisions. There are instances where faith has led to action and there are instances where presumption likened to faith has caused pain.

For example, a pastor I know saw a building for sale for £1.3m. He had £200,000 but believed by faith that God would give them the building, and his church would have it debt-free. He prayed, and in time he went to talk to the owner about selling it at a reduced price so they could use it as a church. The owner wasn't interested. But some time later he decided that he needed a quick sale, so he halved the price to £650,000. The pastor still had just £200,000, but he told his denominational leader that he believed God would give them the building debt-free. The leader mentioned it to a benefactor and told him the story. This man responded by giving the pastor £250,000, and then the very next day the same benefactor increased his gift to enable the pastor to pay the whole £650,000 for the building.

In contrast Pastor Agu of Jesus House tells his own story of how the Jesus House team saw a building in Kilburn, London, and believed it was God's plan for them to own it. They prayed, prayer walked and believed. Pastor Agu even announced to the church that he believed it was the building God would give them. When they found it had been sold to someone else, they were disappointed. Pastor Agu humbly came before the church to apologise and to admit he must have heard wrongly.

Israel Olofinjana

Rev Israel Oluwole Olofinjana is the founding director of the Centre for Missionaries from the Majority World, and an Honorary Research Fellow at Queens Foundation for Theological Ecumenical Education in Birmingham. He is also an ordained and accredited Baptist minister and is the pastor of Woolwich Central Baptist Church, a multi-ethnic, multicultural, inter-generational, inner-city church in south-east London. He pastored Crofton Park Baptist Church from 2007 to 2011, and Catford Community Church from 2011 to 2013. He is a Yoruba Nigerian and comes from a pentecostal background. He holds a BA (Hons) in Religious Studies from the University of Ibadan, Nigeria, and MTh from Carolina University of Theology.

Since 2004 I have had the privilege of leading vibrantly multi-cultural and diverse churches, alongside the challenge of engaging in Bible colleges, festivals and Christian organisations that have been predominantly white. Having felt this tension for a number of years, I'm pleased to say that, more recently, things are starting to improve. It's wonderful to witness networks across the UK beginning to wake up and realise that they have not been engaging with global theologies. This is an entirely necessary move in the right direction on a national level, but it's highlighted the importance for me to keep doing what I can to improve things in my local context as well.

We have 18 to 20 nationalities represented in our congregation. This is a huge blessing for our church, but if we didn't see the same diversity in our leadership then something would be deeply wrong. I was very grateful when I arrived that my predecessor had been intentional about the profile of the leadership accurately representing the demographic of the congregation. I know that, unfortunately, this legacy may not be in place for everyone, but I still felt a tremendous burden to continue cultivating this atmosphere of celebrating multi-culturalism into the future of our church.

One of the key things I focused on when I started was to put diversity at the heart of our church vision. This looked like regularly preaching on it, demonstrating diversity visually from the front – you'd be amazed how many sermon PowerPoints only have pictures of white people – and organising opportunities to celebrate our differing cultures.

Bring-and-share lunches where people bring food from their culture and wear traditional clothing have now become a staple of our community. I've also tried to make sure that we empower people of all ethnicities to serve in every area and at every level of church ministry.

I've learnt that if there are people from different ethnic backgrounds in our churches who aren't growing into leadership then we have to be prepared to ask why. Is it because they haven't got the skills or the confidence, or is it actually because they haven't been given the opportunity? As those already in positions of leadership, we should know the characteristics that we look for in potential leaders, and learn how to spot them in others. This can require seeing through cultural differences and actively seeking out the potential in others, even if they don't see it in themselves.

When I read the Bible, I see diversity from Genesis to Revelation. This may depend on what lens we read the Bible through, but I believe the text itself is still the same: Jews and Gentiles, though different and distinct, are still one in Christ. This means that when we consider diversity in the church, we can't settle for tokenism. One black person on the leadership team isn't enough visible representation, especially in hugely diverse churches. We must keep pursuing authenticity and genuinely desire unity in our diversity. When borne out of a Spirit-fuelled desire, our efforts are much less likely to regress, as can sadly be the case all too often.

Ultimately, what we model in church is also what people carry with them into the rest of the community. I really hope that what we've worked and prayed hard for in our church community will be a blessing to those outside of it as well. As we demonstrate what it means to seek unity in diversity, and to celebrate what makes us different, I pray it would transform a country that doesn't always know how to do that.

Celia Apeagyei-Collins

Rev Celia Apeagyei-Collins is the founder and president of the Rehoboth Foundation, which offers leadership and vision development consultancy, motivational and mentoring programmes, and executive coaching. An award-winning leader, Celia has been listed as one of the top 10 most influential black Christian women in the UK. Among her many roles she is a board member of the One People Commission, a vice president of Tearfund, and a trustee for the International Third World Leaders Association.

I am increasingly coming across church congregations from different ends of the ethnic spectrum that are collaborating on community projects. They are pooling their resources, talents and insight, and filling in the gaps that the other has. One may have the money but doesn't know what to do with it; the other, meanwhile, may have the know-how but lacks finances.

In many ways, this unity for the sake of the communities that God wants us to reach reflects the account of Esther. This Jewish queen of the Persian King Ahasuerus (King Xerxes) had her mouth next to the king's ear, but it was her cousin Mordecai who guided her in preserving the Jewish people. When the two got together, they made history. And that's what I am seeing more and more as Christians across the UK realise that they can't fulfil the will of God in silos.

I have numerous anecdotes of churches working together in this way. But the unity across ethnic groups, and the effectiveness thereof, is not limited to the shared supply of resources. I experience time and time again the united prayers of God's diverse family; faithful, intimate, heartfelt, bold prayers to our Father for His church and those who are yet to know Jesus.

You'll find, for example, that African people typically pray aggressively and are confident in spiritual warfare. This is due to our cultural background; we are spirit and demon aware. But this is not the only type of prayer that is necessary to see God's kingdom come. We find that our Caucasian brothers and sisters' prayers are gentle; they address our Father personally, with the faith of a child, an innocent child, and with kingship in mind.

When we merge, we bring to complete unity our differences. And this is powerful indeed, as it brings about completion. But what do these examples have to do with leadership and teambuilding, and how our leadership needs to change to embrace a new landscape of a more integrated church? A lot. The Bible talks about being in the kingdom for such a time as this. Britain today is incredibly multicultural, and it's not getting less so; in fact, it's becoming even more diverse. Leaders should strive to understand and reflect the political, social, community and church contexts within which they lead.

Those who serve with us must mirror the community we're in. Diversity within leadership is paramount because it's highly likely that if you come from one ethnic background, your cultural awareness might be limited. We need to work with people from different ethnic backgrounds in order to harness what they know about the unique cultural experiences and needs of different communities. How else will we be able to reach these communities? Additionally, when you have a multi-ethnic leadership mix that reflects the community, it tells people they are valued and they matter.

Key principles

1. Whatever your context – church, organisation, network – we need to do more than continue as usual. Rather than ignoring the need for multicultural integration, we need to make it our responsibility to seek visible representation.

2. Focused leadership from the top that delegates down is common in most black ethnic church settings. Whilst leadership in a white British setting tends to be bottom-up, with a collective leadership style. It is important to recognise the cultural differences when serving in different contexts.

3. No leader is called to realise a vision alone; you do it with others.

4. Seeking diversity in your leadership is not about tokenism. A diverse leadership team that reflects and values the local community is best equipped to welcome, influence and serve that community.

Questions

For personal reflection or discussion in your team

1. Where are you and who is with you in your community?

2. How can you work towards creating a multi-ethnic leadership team in your context, so that you are more representative of the people you're trying to engage with?

3. Where could you encourage better visible representation in different areas of ministry or service in your church?

4. What might dissuade a person who is from a different ethnic background putting themselves forward for a role or position of leadership in your context?

5. Are you prepared to input the time, effort and energy that it takes to bring about change when it might mean difficulties, challenges and losing people along the way?

5

Making the Vision a Reality

How do we engage others in a vision of a changed landscape?

STEVE CLIFFORD

Over my time as the general director of the Evangelical Alliance, I have spoken so often from the John 17 prayer of Jesus. I actually began to feel sorry for the staff team who got to hear me yet again picking up the theme of God's passion for the unity of His people. I just couldn't get away from the passage. It's almost as if I have been ambushed by this amazing prayer and the challenge that it brought to us as an alliance, but also, even more significantly, the church right across the UK. Jesus' prayer for the 'oneness' of his people cannot be ignored. It requires our response – whether as an individual, a church, a network of churches, a denomination or a ministry. Interestingly, as I preached on this theme, I can't ever remember receiving an objection. In fact, time and time again, there was an instinctive "amen" or a "yes" with nods of agreement from around the room. It seemed there was universal agreement. I began to realise this thing resonated deeply with the people of God. It was as if the Holy Spirit was witnessing to the theme within the hearts and minds of the congregations.

But, and there is a but, the big question which follows is: Will we do anything about it? The tragedy of history is so often we haven't. We give lip service to the concept of unity, but then we get on with business as usual.

The journey

Turning a vision into a reality doesn't just happen; those of us involved in leadership are aware that vision impartation and ownership requires consistent and focused work. The questions this chapter explores takes us on a journey. How can we take the vision of an ethnically integrated church or organisation and see it become a reality?

Questions to be answered include:

1. Have I captured imaginations?

A God-given vision will not be caught simply because we outline it at a church vision meeting or outline it within a strategy document. It will need repeating again and again and again. Leaders have numerous opportunities to impart vision, and all need to be used in our preaching, teaching and writing, but also in one-to-one conversations; in invitations to others who share this vision from outside to bring their wisdom and input; and in taking people to other churches and organisations who are perhaps further than you are in outworking the vision. For a leader, the aim must be to capture people's imaginations of a new reality. It involves painting a picture of what the future could look like, and for faith to arise across the congregation or organisation, that this is a God-given vision, which we can each play our part in seeing become a reality.

2. Why is this important?

As part of this corporate journey, it will be vital to answer the question, Why is this important?

Some 25 years ago, I would regularly visit Greenford Baptist Church in west London, providing some encouragement and support to the leadership and church. David Wise, the minister, had arrived at this almost entirely white British congregation in 1987 and discovered that it, in no way, reflected the local community. For David, and increasingly his team, this was a situation that needed to be addressed; it was too important to remain as it was. Some years ago, I returned to celebrate a milestone in the church's history. What a different church I encountered, packed with people from more than 45 different nationalities, with no single dominant culture and worship songs in several different languages. I have watched David and, more recently, the current pastor Warren McNeil, intentionally, with great determination and at times facing significant pain and cost, respond to the challenge of seeing a genuinely multi-ethnic church established. For David, this challenge was of vital importance; it required numerous acts of obedience, and a willingness to invest time, energy, prayer, emotional commitment and finances to see a healthy united church, which crossed numerous ethnic backgrounds, being established and flourishing.

3. Is there a story?

As any leader or communicator knows, there is tremendous power in telling a story to communicate a vision. It takes the abstract and makes it concrete and accessible. It's easily remembered and rehearsed to others. A story embeds the vision into the narrative of a church or an organisation. It becomes 'our story', and it honours those who have played their part in the story. In writing his second New Testament book, the Acts of the Apostles, Luke was not embarrassed to tell certain key stories more than once. The conversion of Saul and Cornelius were critical to the future direction of the early church, so their stories needed to be repeated. A story, if rightly told and owned, ensures longevity to the vision: 'It's not going away.' As you've experienced already in reading this resource book, what happened at our 2010 council is not going away. The events that followed are part of the Evangelical Alliance's story in the early years of the 21st century.

4. Can I trust you?

Relationships are the bridge to building trust. When we undermine trust, everything can be lost. Whether in the context of a local church, or between churches or organisations, there is no substitute for relationships. God designed it that way – the Trinity, Father, Son and Holy Spirit are a wonderful interdependent expression of unity, oneness and yet distinction, the essence of diversity. As relationships are nurtured, the bridge is strengthened. Questions, fears, suspicions and insecurities are faced; trust is built, and possibilities begin to emerge. Building trust takes time. Rushing too quickly into a shared project could overstretch the capacity of a bridge, like driving a 20-tonne lorry over a 10-tonne-capacity bridge; the results could be a disaster. Without trust, the danger is a project that is not 'owned', it has simply been 'sold'. One party has been persuaded to be involved, but the emotional and spiritual commitment is low. In a local church, as you will see from examples given by the different contributors to this resource, trust is built as a result of a number of small but intentional steps.

5. What contribution could I make?

For leaders, taking people on the journey from vision to reality must involve an invitation to get involved, not as a passenger, but as an active participant, sharing responsibility, communicating and shaping vision, praying, giving, contributing in both small and large ways.

For the emergence of the One People Commission within the Evangelical Alliance, we are enormously indebted to a wide range of leaders, both BAME and white British, who committed themselves to taking the journey with us. Many of these leaders, who are acknowledged with deep gratitude at the beginning of this book, were to become key champions in the work we were doing. These champions would not only speak well of what we were doing, but would also hold us to account if we failed to stay true to our commitments. For leaders, discovering some God-given champions who will walk alongside us on the journey is often a key.

Champions come in all shapes and sizes. In a local church, they might not be high-profile members of the congregation, but they will be people who have caught the vision and are committed to getting behind it. I remember meeting an elderly member of a church, the church secretary, who with tremendous determination stayed on supporting the new BAME pastor as he established himself in a new congregation and faced the challenge of a very diverse local community. She championed the pastor internally and the church externally, often at great cost.

6. What are the intentional changes we need to make?

One of the earliest questions we realised we needed to ask ourselves at the Evangelical Alliance as we embarked on this journey was: How do we as an alliance need to change in order to reflect the ethnic diversity of the evangelical church in the UK? The answer to that question emerged over a number of years in a multitude of different ways, many of which are outlined in other chapters of this book. While we were clear that God had spoken to us, and we had a vision as to what the future could look like, we also recognised to get there required change, including to our structures, our priorities, how we did things and the personnel involved.

David Wise, arriving at Greenford Baptist Church, recognised that while the church had faithfully served God and the local community for many decades, it was no longer fit for the purposes to which he sensed God had called them. For churches such as this, there are a multitude of adjustments, some high profile, others small and incremental. For the Evangelical Alliance, the appointment of Yemi Adedeji in 2012 as the director of the One People Commission was to prove critical. By that stage Yemi had become a close friend, but he also carried enormous wisdom and credibility across the church scene, both within BAME and white churches. Yemi's input over the past seven years has been crucial in reshaping the Evangelical Alliance's identity and building credibility among the BAME churches.

In March 2016 Dr Tani Omideyi was appointed the board chair of the Evangelical Alliance and thus became my boss. Tani became the first BAME leader to chair the board, which reflected a further step in our journey of integration.

A commitment to ethnic integration will be the challenge of change in numerous settings. For unity movements in towns and cities across the UK, finding ways to build bridges with the ethnic minority churches within their communities, and ensuring they are built into the heart of the movements, will be essential to networks, denominations and agencies. There must be a willingness to embark on the journey of actively recruiting BAME leaders to take up positions of responsibility within their organisation, whether as staff, trustees or leaders. This will of itself carry challenges, but a multi-ethnic leadership team communicates that everyone is welcome. When people can see others who look like them, it encourages them to get involved.

7. Are you committed for the long haul?

As we began this journey of discovery, we quickly realised that if we were serious about this unity challenge, it would require a commitment to the long haul. To use the language of the writer to the Hebrews: "Let us run with perseverance the race marked out for us" (Hebrews 12:1). The race was not a sprint, but was long distance and would require perseverance, persistence, determination and a commitment not to give up.

Running such a race requires:

- Intentional leadership;
- A willingness to learn new skills and knowledge (see the lessons from the journey in Further Reading and Resources);
- Flexibility so that we can adapt on the way;
- Release of resources (people/ money);
- Readiness to give the vision high profile.

In the context of leadership, whether church or organisational, there are likely to be a multitude of decisions, often very small, where intentional decisions can move us in a new direction. Remember, it's a long-distance race, but every step counts.

For leaders embarking on this particular race, resilience in the midst of pressure or conflict is crucial. I've come to realise that most of us, at some stage, when leading an organisation or church, will face the impact of an institution's resistance to change. Institutions of whatever shape or size at some stage begin to take a life of their own, and not only fight for their continued existence, but will resist change

8. Are we praying?

One of the great joys and challenges of the last few years, as I have been exposed to the BAME churches here in the UK, has been their passionate commitment to prayer which is often accompanied by fasting. As I have stood praying in the ExCeL Centre in east London, together with 40,000 mainly Nigerian Christians from the Redeemed Christian Church of God, in a meeting from 8pm in the evening to 6am the next morning, I have been humbled by the depth and passion of prayer, which has been extraordinary and has put much of my own expression of church to shame.

I have come to realise yet again the power of prayer, particularly as we consider vision ownership. It's in the context of prayer that:

- God speaks again and vision is clarified;
- Relationships are strengthened as trust is built;
- Faith grows and belief is challenged;
- Prayers are answered;
- And the enemy is pushed back.

Over the last few years I've come to the realisation that unity across racial backgrounds is a spiritual battleground. If God loves unity, we can be sure we have an enemy who hates all expression of unity across the body of Christ, but particularly in this area. The Apostle Paul exhorts us: "Finally, be strong in the Lord and in His mighty power. Put on the full armour of God, so that you can take your stand against the devil's schemes. For our struggle is not against flesh and blood, but against the rulers, against the authorities, against the powers of this dark world and against the spiritual forces of evil in the heavenly realms" (Ephesians 6:10-12).

He then instructs us to put on the full armour of God to be able to "stand our ground". Looking back, I have come to the conclusion that I didn't take the spiritual battle we had entered into seriously enough as we navigated this journey. Even though the battles had very practical and relational outworkings, it would have helped to see the spiritual dimension to these battles that were taking place, and to mobilise more prayer cover.

9. Can we win the sceptics?

As we have suggested in chapter 1, relationships are the key. If we are in this for the long haul, it is important that we treat the sceptics with respect. In the early days of the One People Commission, it was important that we heard all kinds of concerns, pains from the past and fears as to the steps we were taking. As a leader in such contexts, it is so easy to become defensive. We believe God has spoken to us and we are responding to Him: What's wrong with them? Why can't they see it? Most local church leaders will recognise that when it comes to change, there will be a variety of responses in their congregation. In the business world, the terms 'innovators' (2.5 per cent), 'early adopters' (13.5 per cent), 'early majority' (34 per cent), 'late majority' (34 per cent), 'laggards' (16 per cent) have become common, reflecting the willingness or speed with which a new idea, a new way of doing things, or a change of structure will be embraced. While such theories might be helpful in reflecting personality types, life experiences and educational attainment, care must be taken in remembering we are, as a church, called to be family, recognising each has a contribution to make.

Winning the sceptics (maybe late majority/laggards), even those who are opposed to us, must involve us listening well. We don't have to try to win the argument. Let's face it, winning the argument could result in us losing a friend. Let's also recognise that those with concerns will almost certainly have important points that we can learn from, be challenged by and even respond to by making adjustments. Agreeing to disagree agreeably is not always something we do well in Christian leadership. We have to be willing to take the long view. If God is in this, we can trust Him for the outcome.

Addressing the questions above will not guarantee the success of ethnic integration, but it will provide a route map which will act as a guide on the journey and perhaps at times sustain us on the way.

Dr Tani Omideyi

Tani is the chair of LJM International network of Ministries and Charities he and his wife Modupe have built up over many years and is senior pastor of Temple of Praise congregations.

He is the current chair of board of Evangelical Alliance UK, an Ecumenical Canon of the Liverpool Angelical Cathedral and one of the founding directors of Together for The Harvest, the Liverpool regional unity movement of Evangelical churches.

Tani is a songwriter of more than 100 published worship songs, has a doctorate degree in Chemical Engineering and was for many years a school teacher in a Liverpool comprehensive school.

Over the course of my time in ministry, I've been really impacted both by those who have captured the vision of church that God has given me and also by those who haven't. In each of these instances, God has taught me more about how to engage people with a vision, and I've been reminded that He is always seeking good things for His church in every context.

When I began leading my church in Liverpool, I was a young leader of around 24. I'd started the church in the 1980s in obedience to God's call to plant, following many conversations with people on the streets. We ended up with lots of people from black African descent, and what started as a small house group soon became a lively group of 30 people.

I was so encouraged by the way that black people had responded to the vision of the church from the beginning, joining what was a very early plant, but I felt that God still had more for us as a community. One night, as I slept, I had a dream that God took our house group in His hands and broke it like a loaf of bread, then put it together again. As He did so, the group became mixed with both black and white people.

My background in Nigeria had always been mixed, especially growing up going to a mixed college, so it was something I was used to and fully on board with. I was excited by this vision God had given me and I truly felt that it reflected the heart of the early church at Pentecost. On that day, there were people of all nations, colours and backgrounds, speaking all kinds of languages, but all hearing and responding to the gospel as one. This was exactly what I wanted to see take place in our church in Liverpool.

Unfortunately, as I began to share this vision with the group and ask them to engage, there were some people who walked out. This was a very literal response to the vision I'd had of breaking bread, as some of our group sadly broke away. It was so disappointing that they weren't on board with the direction we were heading in and didn't want the change it would bring, and I found myself asking God, "Okay, what next?" Amazingly, just a few days later, some white men walked into our gathering. Over the course of the following year, many other people joined our group from all different backgrounds and the group began to reflect the integration that I'd prayed for.

The break that had taken place in the church made space for a restructuring of our leadership. It was a really important opportunity to do that at top-level, but I also made the most of that moment to value the sense of family within our church as a whole. I wanted to honour those who had stayed with the new vision, giving them a community where they felt they belonged, and we could all move forward together, even if that involved change. Very quickly the church began spending time together almost every day, creating relationships where racial differences simply didn't matter anymore – something that was very counter-cultural in the 1980s.

Alongside all of this work that God was doing in our church, I always wanted to engage other churches with the multicultural vision I'd had of Pentecost and the call for us to pursue the same thing today. I invited other church leaders to come to our gatherings, which developed relationships across the wider church in Liverpool and reinforced the sense of oneness that we were desperately seeking. Forty or so years later, I am still good friends with several of those church leaders today, and I'm so honoured to have been a part of modelling the power of unity within diversity to our churches, and to our whole city.

Preethy Kurian

Preethy Kurian is one of the Lead Pastors of Capstone Church, a vibrant, spirit-filled, multicultural family of believers. She focuses on impartation and training, to see identity realized, hearts ablaze, spirits revived and lives surrendered to God, walking in victory! With nearly 20 years of joyful service to the Lord, she ministers internationally at various conferences and missions. Preethy was born in India, raised in the Middle East and currently lives in London, UK, with her husband, Rakesh & daughter, Rhema. She is an engineer and the CPO of CrossPay Technology.

When my husband and I moved to the UK in 2005, we quickly felt the heart of the Lord towards east London. Although we'd primarily come to set up a finance and technology business, we began doing street evangelism and prayer. After two years with little visible results, we saw the Lord beginning to move and felt called to plant a church. Today we lead a church of around 25 to 30 nationalities and languages, and it is a privilege to pastor a multi-ethnic community doing life together in God.

Originally from South India, when we first began the plant, most people who joined looked the same as us. It's natural to gravitate towards people like ourselves, but we felt a strong sense that God wanted us to be open to all nationalities, not just our own. This came from the first time we took a group from our congregation on mission to Tanzania, and I told God how excited I was to take people to the nations. I felt God reply: "To you, the nations are geographical boundaries, but to me, they are people. Each one of you carries your nationality with you, and in London, the nations are coming to you!"

This was a mark in the sand for our vision at Capstone Church, and returning from that trip I knew we had to seek God for a blueprint of how to improve in this area. God had called us to incorporate diversity into who we are as a church, so that we could accurately represent the city we were in. Ironically, if we'd stuck to reaching our own community then I knew we would have grown faster, but I had to learn that God is in charge of when His purposes are fulfilled. If we were following His vision for our church, then the timing was up to Him and I had to relieve myself of that pressure.

As we began to live out this vision, there were several cultural quirks that emerged. For example, I'd assumed that everyone prayed the same way, and that the way I prayed was the right way. I discovered that each of us prays as we've been taught in our culture and we need to see different expressions as equally valid. Sometimes we had to reflect on these practices and bring them in line with God's word, but we could never assume that we had all the answers and the way our culture prayed was the only or best way to pray. Much of this took time and learning from observation, but it meant we could pursue a united but diverse model of prayer going forward.

From what I've learnt, in order to bring people on a journey together, you have to do more than just communicate the overall spiritual vision. It is absolutely right to have a clear direction that you're all travelling in, but you have to help people work out which lane they're meant to be running in. Part of welcoming different cultures into our church meant learning things such as people from the Philippines are often phenomenal at honouring people and being hospitable. This meant that within our wider vision, we wanted to create space for them to thrive and bring all that God had gifted them with to our community. We didn't need to change the overall vision, but we did need to put the vision in context so that, within it, every person in our community could flourish and fulfil God's call for them.

When I started out, I honestly felt like I had to know it all. Today, I realise that I don't have to, nor do I even have to pretend to. The church is an organism, not an organisation, and while we must be obedient and focused on God's vision, we should do so with His love and grace.

Anne Calver

Anne Calver is a Baptist minister, author and speaker. She is passionate about combining word and Spirit. She works with Christians from about 30 nationalities in north London, seeing Jesus transform lives and release people's potential. She is married to Gavin and has two children, Amelie and Daniel.

One way we celebrate the ethnic diversity of our church is to have people pray or sing in different languages from the front. There have been occasions where someone from a particular culture has danced during the sung worship and that has been so powerful and memorable. Whenever we seek to release the whole body together in worship to God, the power of the Spirit is more tangible in our services. We do not have all the answers, but we are definitely on a journey, longing to see every tribe and tongue fulfilling the great commission together.

One of the best things our church does is an international evening once a year. There are about 32 nationalities in our church and each person is encouraged to wear their national dress, bring food from their culture, and perform something to display the beauty of their country and their gifts. The first time I was part of this, it made me weep: witnessing the body of Christ being the body, not just in different ages, but in such a spectacularly rich and powerful way. We are so grateful to our Sri Lankan friends for making this event happen. So many people are blessed through this 'togetherness'.

Here are five lessons I've learnt as a white Brit in an ethnically diverse church.

1. Discourage hierarchy. I'm all for everyone serving whether that be in the kitchen, putting out chairs, or clearing away after events. However, in an ethnically diverse church the ministers are not really welcome in these spaces. It is hard to explain to people from some ethnicities the concept of ministers serving as well as preaching and

leading from the front. We do not want to offend or discourage anyone in their role in the body, but we do not want to encourage hierarchy.

2. Include as many different voices as you can around the leadership table. The more ethnically diverse the leadership, the better equipped they are to lead an ethnically diverse church. Shaun Lambert, the senior minister of Stanmore Baptist Church, who I work with, has made this a priority for our church and it is a key value.

3. Language can be a real stumbling block. The speed and the way we communicate can turn off half the congregation early into our talks. I have asked God to give me the ability to communicate in other languages and soon after asking for this, a lady with little English came up after the service saying, through her friend, that she had been able to understand me that morning. What a gift! More, Lord!

4. Clothing matters. Getting outfits right is a challenge on a Sunday morning. I dress far more smartly in our church in north London compared to how I did in an urban deprived white area in a West Midlands church where I trained. If I want to engage the whole congregation I am in heels, smart trousers and a blouse that is not low cut. To be honest, some of our people would rather I was wearing a dress, and others would be happy to see me wearing jeans, so I am on a mission to find the all-encompassing middle-ground.

5. Be aware of unintended consequences. We have café services and constantly question whether or not to serve bacon sandwiches because of who might attend on a Sunday morning. Bacon might feel like a seriously great welcome to a lot of us, but when your church is in a predominantly Jewish area, or with Hindus and Muslims living next door, we might as well write a sign on the door saying "you are not welcome".

We can create so many barriers through food, clothing, language and roles before we have even had a chance to talk about Jesus. Thank goodness for the grace of God and the power of the Spirit, who overcomes all these factors so often because we are truly seeking to love God and one another.

Key principles

1. Capture the imagination using repetition, creative communication and painting a picture of what could be.

2. Look for like-minded people who are willing to learn together. No one needs to be an expert, but we want people to show a willingness to engage with the vision and grow in the right direction.

3. Find the stories that can be told.

4. Be prepared to change what and how you do things in line with the growing vision. You can't put new wine into old wine skins.

5. Disappointment is real and it's okay to feel that. Your community won't change overnight, and not everyone will capture the vision. The key is to keep trusting in God.

6. Keep a watchful eye that the reality of the community you're building is in line with the vision of the church that God has asked you to build. Face issues of trust and look out for cliques and unhelpful behaviour that might impact the culture you want to set in your church.

Questions

For personal reflection or discussion in your team

1. Have you got a story to tell?

2. What are the fears, insecurities or suspicions people will need to face?

3. Who could be the champions?

4. Who could you learn from, and who could you then teach, about what it looks like to pursue this vision of integration?

5. What barriers to ethnic integration exist in your context? Think about each of the ethnic groups of people in your immediate community. Would they be comfortable with the food, clothing and language they'd find in your context?

6. How can you help different people from different ethnic background to understand each other?

6

Making Jesus Known

How do we do evangelism together?

YEMI ADEDEJI

It was a sunny afternoon at London Bridge Station in central London as I watched a team of believers from the BAME community giving out tracts and making an effort to talk to the passers-by. It suddenly occurred to me that they were only reaching out to people who had the same skin colour. I watched for a while before approaching them to ask a question: Why are you selecting a particular colour of people with whom to share Jesus? Why not the rest of the people? The answer I got simply confirmed what I had thought. They did not know how to engage and witness to those who did not look like them.

I guess one could say the same for white British believers who are hoping to reach out to people of diverse ethnic backgrounds. Fear of rejection is the challenge we face when leaving the comfort zone of one's own culture, context and people.

Motivation for evangelism

Jesus commanded: "Therefore go and make disciples of all nations, baptising them in the name of the Father and of the Son and of the Holy Spirit" (Matthew 28:19).

It must surely break Jesus' heart to see the church He founded segregated and separated by colour, ethnicity and class. There has never been a greater tool for evangelism than the witness of ethnically diverse believers that are serving, eating, embracing, fellowshipping and worshipping God together in unity within their community and their local church.

The challenge of integration

A few years ago, a pastor from Nigeria settled in Liverpool and later joined a church that was mainly white British. His involvement and contribution led to him being conferred as the leader of the local church. Not long after, the white congregants started leaving the church and, in a few years, a once-white British majority church turned into a black majority church. The transformation of the church into a BAME church infuriated the white British locals who started an open assault on the church members with arsonist and racist attacks. Sadly, further conversation with the BAME pastor revealed that his position did fuel the neighbours' actions. He believed that he was not called to minister to the white British majority, although he was living and pastoring within the local community. His position was to ignore their existence and the needs of the local community and focus only on the BAME Christians who travelled to the church.

Black man in a white space

It was a different story when I found myself booked into accommodation at the top of a local pub in the middle of rural England while attending a Christian conference. I was asked by the receptionist whether I could read or speak English. It was a smoke-filled, crowded pub with half-drunk white men. I looked different and hated the atmosphere. I warned the receptionist that I would be gone first thing before daybreak. Little did I know that God had something planned. I was irritated and upset, and I found myself condemning and judging the people in the pub. It was in the middle of my lamentation that God reminded me of the past that he had saved me from. Suddenly, I felt a heart of compassion and brokenness, and I went on my knees to pray, asking God for His love for the people in the pub. I made a vow to God that I would complete my four-day stay in the place and would show love instead of condemnation. Two days later, on my return from a seminar at around 2pm, I stopped at the bar to collect the key to my room. It was there that the story took a different turn. I was accosted by one of the locals who questioned me, curious to know what kind of business brought me to their rural local pub. I explained to him that I had come for a Christian conference nearby. That was enough for him to raise his voice and that attracted everyone in the pub. His challenge was specific: I should prove to them that there is a God because most of them didn't think God existed. Being put on the spot, I was going to excuse myself and depart, but then I remembered praying for the people in the pub a few days earlier. I stood back, got myself a non-alcoholic drink and started a conversation. The conversation took a turn when I boldly asked anyone who was willing to become a follower of Jesus to join me in prayer. To my shock, nearly everyone did and 32 grown men in the pub prayed alongside me to receive Jesus as their Lord and saviour.

The arrival of diverse people from across the globe, who are now settled in UK, has made it paramount to consider new ways to make Jesus known and to extend His mission across various ethnic communities.

A joint effort

Mark Deymaz in his book *Building a Healthy Multi-Ethnic Church* (Jossey Bass, 2007) wrote about John 17, that on the night before Jesus died, He delivered the most effective means for reaching the world through the gospel. Surprisingly, He did not ask believers to write books, do crusades, put emblems on cars and bags, or build mega churches for a specific segment of the society. He didn't pray for us to be seeker-sensitive, post-modern, emerging or a purpose-driven church. Jesus without doubt called us to be one, because it is only in being united as one that the world will know God's love and then believe.

In an effort to explore evangelism from a diverse ethnic expression with a unified purpose, my friend Gavin Calver, the newly appointed chief executive of the Evangelical Alliance, and I decided to do a joint sermon on reaching the lost from diverse ethnic and host churches. After all, how else will people know that the message of salvation crosses ethnic boundaries and backgrounds? Gavin is white British. His passion to reach the lost is infectious. Our content when doing a joint preaching engagement focuses first on the love we both have and demonstrate for each other, before sharing our experiences and practical tips on doing evangelism through a diverse lens.

The commandment preceded the mission

Some specific biblical narratives have helped shape my personal engagement in mission and evangelism. I am of the opinion that the commandment of God preceded the mission of God. Jesus sums up Moses' 10 Commandments when asked by a teacher of law: "Of all the commandments, which is the most important?" (Mark 12:28).

"'The most important one', answered Jesus, 'is this: 'Hear, O Israel: The Lord our God, the Lord is one. Love the Lord your God with all your heart and with all your soul and with all your mind and with all your strength.' The second is this: 'Love your neighbour as yourself.' There is no commandment greater than these'" (Mark 12:29-31).

The first step in doing the mission of God is to be in love with God. An outcome of one's love of God must then be expressed in our love for our neighbours. This may refer to those who do not look, smell, dress, act or talk like us. Every authentic mission must emanate from a heart of love. Love is a powerful tool and love always compels us to give and sacrifice our best in an effort to embrace others.

A few years ago, I was travelling in a taxi with my white British colleagues in the north of England. My colleagues watched and listened as I started an impromptu conversation with the taxi driver on various issues. Most importantly, I showed genuine concern for him and the situations he was facing. He was shocked by an expression of love from a black person travelling with white colleagues. Our conversation had a twist, as I asked him what he thought about the person of Jesus. He later agreed to an offer of prayer and expressed a desire to become a follower of Jesus. Nothing compares to the power available when leaving one's comfort zone to share the good news.

The Apostle John quoted Jesus in John 13:34-35: "A new command I give you: love one another. As I have loved you, so you must love one another. By this everyone will know that you are my disciples, if you love one another."

Love creates the platform for mission to be activated

Whenever my friend Gavin speaks to a mainly BAME audience, he always focuses on how our love for each other has inspired our passion to witness and demonstrate God's love, and how such love should motivate people to reach out to their neighbours and the communities that don't look like them.

Having spent the vast majority of my time as a missionary both with the white British and the diverse BAME churches, I have discovered that humility, love and contextualisation are needed to embrace the changing landscape of UK communities.

Though the BAME Christian sees evangelism as an integral part of their ministry, the majority are culturally and socially handicapped on how to effectively engage and reach out to the host community. The host Christian community equally sees mission and evangelism as vital, but many have found it challenging. When engaging with the diverse ethnic communities, some feel it is necessary to apologise first for the way they have treated people from different ethnic communities, demonstrating a 'saviour mentality' which is often seen as a sign of 'white privilege' mentality.

Methods of evangelism

Missional issues

Most mono-ethnic churches are currently facing minimal growth or sharp decline with few exceptions. The members are ageing, the young generations are leaving, and only those who are intentionally missional are bending the curve.

Recently, I was asked by an African pastor to give advice on the difficulty he is facing in doing mission in his local white British community, and also to help find ways to retain the few locals that visited once but never came back.

I have also been asked to advise a white Anglican vicar in south-east London, the home of a large BAME community, who is finding pastoring a church of diverse ethnicities a challenge particularly because of the flight of the few white British Christians in the church.

I also recently attended a Korean church leaders' event. They specifically wanted me to advise them on how to start integration, since the majority of their meetings only reproduce what is acceptable back home.

Emerging generation

There is no doubt that there are thousands of diverse ethnic minority communities from different nations doing successful ministries across UK. The challenge is not in the growth of their ministries but in the integration of such ministries with other diverse people groups. The same could be said about the ministries of the host community. Until recently it was easier to grow mono-cultural ministries that reach out to a specific people group or culture. Now the landscape has changed dramatically. Second and third generation migrated communities now see themselves as fully-fledged British and there has been a steep rise inter-racial marriage. According to the 2011 census, the number of dual heritage children up to four years old rose from 116,000 in 2001 to 220,000 in 2011. As churches we need to be equipped for multicultural ministry.

Prayer and resources

It's a fact that most BAME Christians see evangelism and mission from the lens of prayer and action, while the host community sees mission and evangelism as a structured process that might include the publication of resources, conferences, seminars, research studies, reports and presentations.

I was recently asked to join a team of speakers to encourage church leaders on church planting. I noticed that the majority of the talks were intellectual, structured, and presented with PowerPoint slides. I really enjoyed them all, but I am also conscious that as a BAME Christian strategic prayers and fasting are also needed to help church planting. Talking to the church leaders about spiritual warfare, and leading them into such prayers, was alien to them but greatly appreciated.

Confidence in the gospel

Many BAME communities, particularly those from Africa and Asia, have an understanding of a god because many have come out of syncretism, animism and other expressions of religion. Their conversion experiences to become followers of Jesus are often dramatic and inspiring and they tend, therefore, to be passionate, loud and intense in their style of witnessing. They have an understanding of a god and are energised when they come to know Jesus as their Lord and saviour. The expression of their faith and witness can appear as being judgemental and strong, which might put off a reserved white British community that has little or no understanding of a god.

It is a common phenomenon for BAME churches to dedicate specified days every month to evangelism. A day where most church members are encouraged to go into the church neighbourhood and high street to distribute tracks and knock on doors. As positive as this process might look, it is clearly productive back home in places like Africa, but the approach has not resulted in church growth in Britain. Most white British people want to belong before they believe. They simply want to be loved before God's word is communicated to them. I learnt a simple method from my friend Gavin. Imagine the amount of time we spend eating out, meeting people and being served by waiters in restaurants. His style has become a guide for me because it works. Simply ask the waiter whether he or she has something pressing that needs prayers while waiting for the order. I have found this simple act useful and effective.

It is true that many people have a strong desire to love people from different ethnic and cultural backgrounds, but they do not know how to go about it because of the fear of going against the law or being accused wrongly. The resource *Speak Up,* produced by the Evangelical Alliance, and *Talking Jesus,* produced by HOPE Together, have been an enormous support, giving Christians confidence to share the gospel.

Social action

Social action has become the arrowhead that has helped to open up communities or people groups prompting conversations that deal with their socio-economic situation. This has become a bridge for many churches to reach their communities. From a church point of view and from the example of the life of Jesus in the Bible, the remit for social action is with the sole purpose of glorifying God and positioning the local church as the solution to the complexity and problem of the community. Organisations like Christians Against Poverty, Foodbank and Street Pastors have helped incredibly to create ready soil to activate evangelism.

Storytelling

If you don't tell your story no one will know what has been done, and no one will attribute the good deeds to you, and no one will ever know how to thank God for what He has done. Giving testimonies has become part of the liturgy of the African churches, and it is a singular initiative that proves and demonstrates the power of God and witnesses to the saving grace of God, irrespective of ethnicity. A good story is always an encouragement to inspire others and gives them a second wind to push forward. If you are struggling to be noticed in your sphere of ministry, simply tell your story. If you want more people to find out about God, tell your story.

You need to let the world know who you are and what you are doing. "Let your light shine before others, that they may see your good deeds and glorify your Father in heaven" (Matthew 5:16). Telling your story makes you accountable to the people you have told, because the light will be on you as a leader as an example to others. People will watch out for what you do next to inspire them.

Telling your story gets you noticed and makes you attractive to others. No one wants to associate with those who are going nowhere; everyone wants to associate with those who are making things happen.

Britain: the new mission field

There is no doubt that Britain has become a mission field for many Christian migrants from across the world. Many Christians from the diaspora see themselves as missionaries on reverse mission to the UK. There are certain characteristics that are evident in the Christian migrants that are culturally alien to the white British population. As alien as these actions may be, they express boldness and passion for their love of Christ. For example, the BAME community will publicly and loudly give credit to Jesus without apology, while it may not be so for a white British Christian. In some instances, it will be culturally acceptable to be bold about one's faith as a BAME Christian, while public displays of faith may be challenging for a white British person. I can recollect many instances when I have been encouraged by my white British colleagues to say some things while speaking in a public space because they couldn't say the same thing without being heavily criticised. To them, it's acceptable since I'm from the BAME community. I believe white British Christians can learn from the confidence and boldness seen in BAME communities.

What next?

In trying to explore practical ways of engaging in mission and evangelism across different ethnic divides, we must explore the current challenges and those that will come in the future. The future and growth of BAME churches can no longer be through immigration; it must be through integration and contextual evangelism.

The white British churches must also be clear about deliberately choosing to engage the emerging, young BAME Christians as joint leaders with equal responsibility and position. The danger in the future is to lose the BAME Christians if inclusion does not lead to seamless integration.

To effectively launch cross-cultural and multi-ethnic evangelism, it's important to:

- Read the culture
- Love the people
- Overcome prejudice
- Listen to God
- Listen to the people
- Explore opportunities to make Jesus known

Richard Anniss

Richard and his wife, Judith, are the senior leaders of King's Church in Greater Manchester, as well as being part of the Core Team for Pioneer UK. Richard joined King's Church shortly after arriving in Manchester as a student back in 1993. He fell in love with both the church and the city (as well as Judith who he met there!) and he has been there ever since. With its central location in the heart of the city, right next door to two Universities, the church has always had a large multi-cultural element. Richard and Judith are white British but the leadership team, like the church, is culturally diverse.

We have to start from a place of knowing and believing that in Christ we are one. We're not trying to become one. We don't become one by trying to deny or even blend our differences. We believe the gospel that Jesus has made us one in Christ, and then we work from that starting point.

I think it's okay to value different cultures and to celebrate our diversity while still being deliberate about the specific culture(s) we feel we are called to reach out to as a church. At King's Church we want to find ways of celebrating and valuing our diversity, whilst still remaining relevant and accessible to the mainstream 21st-century culture of Greater Manchester, whatever that may be. For us, this means some of the cultures that are strongly represented amongst us being willing to accept that we don't 'do church' the way they were used to back home, as it would probably feel less accessible to most of the population of our city. Additionally, from experience, it might also feel less relevant and accessible to their own children who are growing up here.

We all have a tendency to think that only other people have a culture and that what we do is 'normal', just like we sometimes think that only other people have accents and that we speak normally and are easy to understand. I've learned that I have a culture and that some people find it difficult to understand me. The more I've realised how strange some of the ways I behave must seem to other people, the more I've learned to be patient with cultural differences.

I've learned to really value people's cultures by showing as much interest as I can, and learning as much as I can about them. We have a lot of Nigerians in our church so on one occasion I accepted an invitation to visit a number of churches in Nigeria. I ended up preaching and teaching at various church meetings but, for me, the main purpose of going was to learn more about some of the people I am called to lead and to understand better the culture and experience that has shaped them. I definitely came home with a deeper understanding and with more patience for some of the things that I find more difficult to appreciate.

We've learned to have honest conversations about cultural differences so that we can learn from and accommodate and those things that might be less helpful. I think the more we've shown appreciation for the different cultures that are represented, the easier it's been to say that there are some things we don't feel we can embrace. I've learned to be open, honest and vulnerable when talking about culture. I've learned that we don't really deepen our understanding, or discover our blind spots, when we hide behind the things we feel we're supposed to say or shy away from awkward conversations. We need to be patient and gracious but determined to learn from one another. I think it helps if we start from a point of knowing that we are brothers and sisters, but accept that we've still got a lot to learn about one another.

It also helps when I mention twice as many downsides to my own culture as anything I'm trying to address in another person's. I often start by asking people if they find white British people cold, disinterested and stand-offish and assure them that we don't mean to come across that way and that we do really care. One thing that we found quite helpful in addressing this in a church meeting was when my Nigerian colleague, Kofo, and I preached a joint message together where we laughed at our differences and the ways in which we can misunderstand each other.

Les Isaac

Rev Les Isaac OBE is CEO of Ascension Trust. Born in Antigua, Les moved to the UK when he was six years old and experienced gangs and street violence. He became a Rastafarian in his search for hope and in his late teens he became a Christian. This radical, life-changing experience inspired him to seek ways to engage with the same hard-to-reach communities that he came from. Les is committed to sharing not only the spiritual relevance of the gospel message of Jesus Christ but also its very practical message.

I recently had a meal with a chap who I hadn't seen properly for 18 months. In the years leading up to that reunion, we would regularly meet up on a Sunday night and eat and drink together. During these occasions, we would open up, sharing our heart's desires and our disappointments; we'd also pray together.

Due to the genuine relationship we developed over the years, if we don't see each other for a long period of time, when we do eventually meet up, it's as if no time had passed at all. We have a deep relationship.

For several years I have been meeting with a group of Anglican church leaders at 6.30am on Thursdays to pray. This time of fellowship has brought us into a relationship that stretches beyond the types of professional relationship that exist among some Christian and church leaders.

We are brothers and sisters in Christ, and our dedication to understanding each other and nurturing these relationships facilitates God's Spirit as He draws us closer to each other. It's not uncommon for me to walk past the church garden of one of the Anglican ministers during a BBQ, smell the food and pop in, unannounced. I am welcomed, and if there's something on my heart troubling me about the country, I can share it with him. The same is true with the others, and they receive the same welcome from me.

I give these examples because I believe relationship, food and fellowship are at the heart of us working across ethnicities and cultures to make Jesus known. You cannot achieve anything without relationship, getting to know people's character, worldviews, individuality.

Food helps us to develop relationships with one another; it's quite incredible that an informal meal is a setting in which people feel confident and say what they really mean, where they can both agree and disagree. Fellowship strengthens relationships, too. By fellowship, I don't just mean sharing each other's pulpit; I mean worshipping and praying together.

If we do those things, it really helps us. It's helped me. Those three things underpin my relationships with leaders, and we've done amazing things together. Before I started Ascension Trust, I approached some close friends, Christian leaders, who I had fellowship with, and spoke to them about starting an organisation that would help the church engage in cross-cultural mission, particularly in the urban context.

Ascension Trust's footprint is now not only urban, but all over the UK – in the suburbs and rural areas, too. We also have a footprint in Australia and different parts of America, where we're sending members of our team who are from African, Caribbean and South Asian backgrounds to different parts of the world.

The same is true for Street Pastors; it's rooted in relationships. Since I set up the initiative in 2003, it has helped thousands of people. I recall the prison governor of HM Prison Brixton asked for a street pastor on every wing because most inmates had had a positive experience with our team.

The challenge for many Christian and church leaders is to move away from the event culture that we have developed, where the only time we meet is at an event, and develop relationships that have real depth.

Key principles

1. When Jesus prayed for us, His priority was that we would be one, so the world could know God's love.

2. The ability to work together across ethnicities and cultures to make Jesus known is made possible through first developing genuine relationships with each other.

3. Find ways to build confidence in the gospel and boldness in sharing it effectively and relevantly across ethnic divides.

4. Strategic prayers and fasting are vital prerequisites for evangelism and church planting.

5. It takes time, persistence and will to build relationships with Christians that can lead to effective, collaborative evangelism.

Questions

For personal reflection or discussion in your team

1. What are your church's priorities and motivation for evangelism?

2. What is your own culture like and what might be some negative characteristics of it?

3. What are the positive characteristics of cultures, other than your own, in your community?

4. How could you expand your horizons to reach out to people outside your comfort zone?

5. What changes would make your church more accessible to the cultures you are called to reach?

6. How can you change your planning processes to give priority to prayer and fasting?

7. How can you use food and fellowship to develop and enhance relationships with church, Christian and community leaders?

7

Worshipping as One

How can we use music to more effectively engage with those around us of differing ethnic backgrounds?

Anu Omideyi

Anu Omideyi is director of Our Songs International. Anu is a choir director, worship leader, vocal coach and songwriter who leads worship, trains worship teams, directs choirs, writes songs, and conducts vocal training in a variety of Christian and non-Christian settings. She works with all denominations and ethnic backgrounds. She is black British of African descent.

Nicky Brown

Nicky Brown was brought up in the Church of God in Christ with its rich tapestry of pentecostal word and music. His mother was an evangelist who gave him access to a wealth of American gospel music, which she brought back from her travels to the US. This has produced a musician, producer and composer who is also the minister of music under the leadership of Bishop John Francis, founder and senior pastor of Ruach Ministries. Nicky is British of African Caribbean descent.

O'Neil Dennis

O'Neil Dennis is chief editor for the gospel music website aStepFWD. He founded the site as a young Christian wanting to listen to UK gospel and Christian music. aStepFWD's very own UK chart showcases the best in UK Christian music.

hat a fantastic journey Christian and gospel music has had in the past few years. So many new sounds, heartfelt lyrics and inspired songs reflect the Bible and God's own heart.

In every area of society, diversity is at the forefront of the conversations like never before, and we have certainly experienced this first-hand. Between us, we've led or engaged in worship in churches of all sizes and from several denominations, traditions and ethnic backgrounds such as Church of England, pentecostal, evangelical, Catholic, black majority led, white majority led, Spanish, Asian...the list goes on. We continue to find that when combined with the right intentions and focus, the impact of music in worship is phenomenal, helping us connect to God and with His people. At times we have not even understood the language being sung or spoken in congregations where we are ministering, but we have been stirred in our spirits and drawn closer to God.

When God's people from diverse ethnic background focus on Him and express themselves in worship, it demonstrates the unity we will experience when we come before God's throne as that "great multitude...from every nation, tribe, people and language" (Revelation 7:9).

Even as singers, songwriters and musicians up and down the country continue to press on musically, to higher heights and greater depths, there are still many questions to continue pondering. How can we use music more effectively to engage with those around us of differing ethnic backgrounds? Are we investigating the musical sounds from diverse cultures and ethnicities? How can we engage local residents through music in our churches?

Bring glory to God together

We believe music is important to any church service, whether through hymns, worship songs, liturgy set to music, choruses or any type of sacred musical offering. Sunday services are a time when people can come together to glorify God and sing their shared testimonies through songs. It's a time to blend our voices into one, directing our sung worship as an offering to God in fellowship with each other.

As a reputable choir director and worship leader, Anu is no stranger to working with people of diverse backgrounds. She says: "Everywhere I go I find that people respond passionately to music. I have also been very fortunate to lead worship at different churches, conferences and Christian gatherings, with very different congregations in various different environments. I grew up, and still worship, in a black-majority congregation with a strong African influence. But ministry and work has taken me to Caucasian congregations with not a single black person in sight, to Asian congregations, South American congregations, and to European churches. In all these situations, whether at a primary school or in a Bengali-speaking church, the challenge is always well defined: how do I connect with the people? If I'm leading worship in an environment that doesn't mirror my appearance, upbringing or cultural style, I'm acutely aware that the congregants will come with their own expectations, experiences and measures for impact.

"I find that people connect more easily with God when several factors combine to create familiarity: the lyrics and language of the song; its melody; the accompaniment or chord patterns played by the instrumentalists; the rhythm or beat of the song; the mix of musicians in terms of gender and ethnicity, and so on. When one or more of these factors combine, it creates familiarity which can be an effective method to process what is happening as it brings comfort, inclusivity and promotes belonging, all of which makes it easier to grasp the message and the impact of the worship."

Possibilities

Have you tried:

- Introducing one new musical piece that embraces a single aspect of a different culture once or twice a month – it could be completely transformative after a while.
- Introducing a single aspect of a different culture that could be as simple as taking a well-known hymn or song and singing a verse in a different language or using a different cultural rhythm to accompany the song.
- Seeking out a brand-new song emanating from a minority group in the church or in the community, and introducing it into the worship roster.
- Variations of, or all of the above?

These very simple measures can ensure that the participants hold some form of ownership and connection with the worship. Whilst it would be impossible and perhaps inappropriate to ask every member of the congregation for their favourite song, if the leadership is intentional about reflecting its local community, as well as its church community, it would assist in evangelising people from these communities.

Prepare for worship

Anu explains how she prepares to lead worship in churches where they don't speak or sing in English at all. She says, "In preparation for my sessions I ensure that the songs and music I use are familiar to them, and are something they would connect with and respond to. Any new material has to be simple, easy to catch on to, transferable to their context, and close to what they already know. My greatest concern is always making sure they understand the message in the music and feel the power in the songs. Apart from the human research, I always rely on the Holy Spirit as my greatest guide.

"I also make sure I participate in the services from start to finish, not just when ministering, even if I can't understand a word spoken or sung. Sometimes I ask for a translator from the congregation or I grab onto every word and Bible passage I can decipher, as well as following in the Spirit. This is important to me as it means I'm in tune with what God is doing in the service before it's my turn to minister and also after, as I'm often called back later. It is important for the congregation to see the effort to worship with them and not just perform for them. It makes a massive difference!

Here are four key principles to help you prepare to lead worship in a new context:

- Never assume every congregation will receive what you 'normally' do. Find out ahead of time what they do or connect with.
- Read the temperature of the room before you minister.
- Make every effort to participate genuinely alongside the congregation before and after ministry, so you are in tune with what is already happening when you minister. There's nothing worse than ministering on topic 'C' when the meeting is focused on topic 'A'. It's harder to connect!
- People respond better when they know you've tried to integrate even a small aspect of their culture. So even if you change one line of a song to the language of the congregation, they'll be touched by it, which will make it easier to receive the ministry you're giving.

Aim for excellence

Renown gospel music producer Nicky Brown recently worked with Hillsong in London, which is a great example of a multi-ethnic and multicultural community. When asked why he was called in, Nicky said: "In order to be totally relevant you always have to look outwards and broaden your experiences and knowledge. In a content-rich world we have to be good at what we do to compete for people's time. The only way we can compete with televisual and online presentations is with excellence. A bad audio system, bad sight lines, loud instruments, and uninformed, unconnected or unintelligible content, doesn't engage people.

Being the best isn't important, but always striving to present our best moves us towards improvement, enjoyment and excellence. Even a small church with limited resources can enable the whole congregation to express themselves in worship which includes expressions from diverse ethnicities.

If in doubt, keep it simple. Music is important, but presentation trumps performance every time. I'd rather see a good simple set well presented, than a great, all bells and whistles, super-loud, unorganised, over-indulgent talent show that excludes worship and leaves no space for the listeners or participants.

Broaden your experience

Never feel that discovery, relearning or experiencing new things intentionally for inspiration aren't important; the experiences will be enriching even if they don't become a part of your 'everyday' arsenal.

Don't be afraid to take advice, invite people in and expose yourself and your music teams to new and colourful things or disciplines. Bringing in experts to help in specific areas isn't a sign of failure but a way of informing and educating your music team. Even if you do something well, you can always do it better.

Music can be polarising as well as inclusive so think carefully about the trans-generational aspects. Think about your congregation and what you'd like them to be introduced to, as well as what they may like. Put the two together to develop worship sessions that include rather than exclude.

All music can be God's music: gospel, contemporary Christian music, hymns – whether cultural or traditional – with different rhythms and style can all express God's heart. Who are we to decide what He moves through?

Harness God-given gifts

Through his work with aStepFWD, the multi-generational, multi-media organisation that powers an independently run national UK Christian Chart, O'Neil has encountered hundreds of musicians who have already taken great time, money and effort to develop their new sounds into songs. Whilst many of these are not for congregational use, they demonstrate the ever-apparent desire of the 'ordinary' church member to harness their God-given gifts for the wider church or world at large.

With hundreds of artists and thousands of songs informing the musical landscape, it is a most exciting time to be involved in helping to shape the worship in our churches and our communities for maximum positive impact. Appreciating what distinguishes us, whilst celebrating what unites us, is a sure way of fostering unity.

Leaders and influencers have the awesome responsibility of creating a healthy environment and fostering real change, as the world progressively becomes a more diverse place to live. Our musical tastes have been shaped by the environment we grew up in. Facilitating and encouraging greater tolerance of differing musical styles and genres will create a better legacy for those coming behind us who will live in an even more diverse human landscape.

As leaders:

- Be consistent in exposing those around you to different musical and cultural expressions as often as you can.
- Be mindful of intergenerational differences, and be specific in your targeting, rather than assuming all people like all styles of music even in worship.
- Remember that children and families, socialising, identity, location and life experiences all help to drive our demand for culture. Explore ways of weaving music into all of these over time.
- Have a plan to engage and to educate as you integrate different ethnicities. Music can be a powerful tool as part of this process.

Key principles

1. Find ways to incorporate your local communities' musical style into your worship music. Get your congregation used to the idea of having a progressive mindset towards music and worship, by introducing new songs on a regular basis.

2. Introduce or create the signature voice or sound that God releases to your church. Worship leaders/choirs/musicians should seek to understand the spiritual direction that their leaders are travelling so they can create relevant music that reflects the unique journey of your church.

3. Be mindful of the needs of your congregations with regard to resources. What steps are required to make it easier for the congregation to engage and integrate? Excellence is achieving one's best within one's means.

4. Help to celebrate your congregation's heritage. Remember the hymns and songs of the past and find ways to incorporate intentional learning of these and of the prayers of our fathers.

5. Worship in Spirit and in truth is the most potent force and should never be compromised.

Questions

For personal reflection or discussion in your team

1. Are we making it easy for people who don't speak our language to understand what's going on?

2. Do we have translators who are readily available?

3. Can we incorporate a new song with a different language bi-monthly or quarterly or even monthly?

4. Have we asked the ethnic minority groupings in our church if there's a favourite song they'd like to incorporate into worship?

5. Have we made space to incorporate styles and sounds of worship that don't sound or look like ours?

8

Learning from Generational Differences

How do we connect with young adults of different ethnicities?

YEMI ADEDEJI

As a father of British-born millennials, who are of African origin, I am keenly aware of the pressures and the realities of their experiences, views about church, ministry, family, and work and social lives. The question most leaders, irrespective of ethnicity, are asking themselves across the country is how to make the church relevant and participatory for young adults from a different and diverse ethnic mix.

I was approached by a pastor friend who had migrated from another country and culture to the UK. He wanted to know why the young people in his church didn't carry a paper Bible, appeared uninterested in his sermon, were always half asleep during his 9am service, and most importantly looked casual and informal in their dress when coming to church. To make matters worse for him, his own children had started going to another church since attending university. Most parents lose the parental and cultural connection they have with their children once they are off to university. Freedom from parental control, an exposure to liberal thinking, a liberated British lifestyle, and social media have disconnected most young people from their home culture, family and church life. Though this may be more prevalent with those who are exposed to a new world at university, nevertheless, those who don't go to university are similarly influenced by the prevailing culture and the media.

My pastor friend's story is not unusual. Most leaders are concerned that they have lost the ability to connect with young adults and particularly those from diverse ethnic backgrounds.

In the early years of my appointment as the director of the One People Commission at the Evangelical Alliance, the subject of young adults, faith and the church was at the top of the list of concerns with church leaders. This led to research that was carried out on 'Building Tomorrow's Church Today', which can be downloaded from the Evangelical Alliance website. The research among young adult Christians, aged 18-37 and living in the UK, revealed interesting results about young adults, ethnicity and church.

The research showed that white British young adults are more than twice as likely to say that their ethnicity is not important to their sense of identity, while half of BAME young adults say that their ethnicity is essential to their identity. Further study revealed that only 37 per cent of BAME young adults identify fully with their parents' cultural background compared to 49 per cent from the white British community. For BAME young adults in the UK, the generational link to parental culture seems to be declining more and more as the years pass.

Over the years we have gathered young adults from different ethnic backgrounds at forums to explore these issues and other concerns around integration. Digging deeper we have found that only a few leaders understand the struggle and the diverse differences between the British-born BAME, foreign-born BAME and white British young adults. For second and third generation BAME young adults living and working in UK, there is tension around being BAME at home and fully British outside home. Only a few leaders understand the needs and concerns of young adults. Those who do are now creating space for the emerging leaders and bridging the gaps.

In recent years many BAME millennials (those born between 1981 and 1996) and Generation Z (born between 1995 and 2015) have attended white British Christian festivals like Soul in the City, Spring Harvest and New Wine. It's amazing to see how many young BAME Christians have now made a charismatic white British church their home church. Unfortunately, most BAME churches are currently losing many of their young people, except those few who have adjusted to the needs and the concerns of the emerging generation.

It's encouraging to know that this challenge is not new. King David wanted to build a temple for the Lord, but he was halted by God. His role was to prepare the resources and create the space for his young son Solomon to build the temple.

"David said, 'My son Solomon is young and inexperienced, and the house to be built for the Lord should be of great magnificence and fame and splendour in the sight of all the nations. Therefore I will make preparations for it.' So David made extensive preparations before his death. Then he called for his son Solomon and charged him to build a house for the Lord, the God of Israel" (1 Chronicles 22:5–6).

Why did God want young Solomon to build the house instead of his father David?

"David said to Solomon: 'My son, I had it in my heart to build a house for the Name of the Lord my God. But this word of the Lord came to me: You have shed much blood and have fought many wars. You are not to build a house for my Name, because you have shed much blood on the earth in my sight'" (1 Chronicles 22:7–8).

This passage brings a great challenge to the older generation. Can they see beyond the present and build into the future? In many ways this text appears like an instruction to older leaders across ethnicities. It seems as if God requires the older church leaders to put together resources, support and guidance that will help the emerging young leaders to build a house that will not have the shed blood of prejudice, racism, seclusion and separatism – a house that is unified, showing diversity, inclusion and authentic integration.

I was at a packed Sunday church service one day with a pastor friend of mine and thousands of people giving thanks to God. But my pastor friend was looking dejected and sad. He bent over towards me and said, "This is the beginning of our decline; if we don't do something now, we will start a rapid decline." I was perturbed. Wasn't I seeing thousands of people dancing and praising God? He asked me to gauge the age range of the people. There was a noticeable absence of the emerging generation and people from the white British community. I could not but agree with him; the church was mono-ethnic and made up of the older generation. Where were the younger generation and people from the host community? I have no doubt that this situation has also become a common phenomenon in numerous white British churches. So, what can be done to bridge the gap?

Worldview

Amongst the older generation Bible-believing Christians, evangelical beliefs are largely orthodox, but many from the emerging generation experience doubts with their faith. Although these doubts are less common among young adult BAME Christians compared with white British Christian young people, there is a wide variety of opinions on ethical and theological issues such as the inerrancy of the Bible, evolution, hell, homosexuality, cohabiting, marrying non-Christians, abortion and assisted dying. These issues are complex and confusing for the emerging generation. Only a few BAME and white British leaders are brave enough to open up conversations on these subjects, to name the elephant in the room and speak openly about them. In many instances it's almost taboo for a younger BAME Christian to challenge the position of the church or question the teaching of their leaders. Tolerance is at an all-time low compared with white British leaders, who might be more accepting and open to dialogue and conversation.

Since culture plays a significant role in the divergence of opinion, it is important for leaders to understand the new normal and the prevailing worldview of young leaders from both the BAME and the white British backgrounds. Leaders who are prepared to create forums that welcome open dialogue to consider the challenging and counter-cultural 'why' questions from younger leaders will ultimately make the difference.

Leadership

In the *Building Tomorrow's Church Today* research study carried out on the views and experiences of young adults and the church, only 40 per cent of white British Christians attending a church, where others are predominantly of the same ethnicity, developed their leadership skills compared to 52 per cent of those attending an ethnically diverse church. But the story is different when compared to BAME Christians attending a church where others are predominantly of the same ethnicity. In this context, 59 per cent claim they are given an opportunity to develop leadership skill as compared to only 30 per cent of those attending a church where others are predominantly of a different ethnicity to them. It appears as if the BAME young adults are more easily absorbed into leadership roles within their own community compared to a mixed-ethnic context, while the result is the opposite for white British young adults.

For example, a black British man once asked for my advice on his journey to become an ordained minister within the established church. He was attending a white British church which he had made his home church over many years. He had a desire to explore the ministry but was not given the necessary support to explore his gifts. He was asked to wait and watch until such an open opportunity opened. He expressed his frustration at the glass ceiling he was facing. I advised him to explore using his gift to serve and grow in a mixed fellowship that was a majority BAME community. I was not surprised when I saw him next. He had blossomed, and is now on the way to being ordained into a full-time ministry.

One thing is particularly interesting to note from the study: 73 per cent of both BAME and white British young adults claim that they connect more with God when attending an ethnically diverse church. Leaders should pay attention to the key concerns of young adults, responding to them and encouraging them to take leadership roles, which will allow them to help the church to become more ethnically diverse, inclusive and integrated.

Hierarchical structures

It's cultural for most BAME leaders to operate a hierarchical structure that limits the involvement and contributions of young leaders. Most leadership teams, pastoral councils and trustees do not have younger people as contributors or members who help shape the future. Involvement at this level is mostly based on age, seniority, title and how long someone has been in the church. It's no surprise that the majority of young adults have left their churches, when the older leaders make decisions that affect the younger generation without having their voice in the room. Engaging young adults in leadership roles will help model a new pathway for any church.

Information changes everything

Facts, figures and Google – the world of information has demystified myths and the fables of old that inform older leaders. Leaders who cannot support a directive with facts leave themselves open to be challenged by the young ones. This is particularly difficult for most BAME leaders who have grown up in a culture where leaders are never challenged. Now they are being exposed to a new world that asks for proof and evidence. The younger generation wants to know Why? before What?

Will my gifts and talents make a difference?

Seventy per cent of the BAME young adults agree that their continuous service in a church is guaranteed where their skills and service are used to serve God. While only 48 per cent of white British young adults would say the same, 62 per cent say they want to use their gifts to serve in an ethnically diverse church. It is important for integration and the future face of the church that the diverse gifts of young adults are acknowledged, irrespective of age and ethnicity. Young adults will make a visible impact when given space to dream, do the ground work and own an initiative.

The younger generation is often passionate about causes such as the environment, justice and mission.

Their desire to make a difference to their world can be harnessed in local and global mission, advocacy and the pursuit of justice. Many are prepared to get involved in projects, initiatives and events together with their friends and colleagues across ethnic divides. They might choose causes that don't easily resonate with the older generation, but which can be excellent vehicles for inclusion and integration. They need permission to lead, freedom to be creative, and support to use their gifts and talents to make a difference.

Reverse mentoring leadership

I was at a church when the pastor had delegated leading the meeting to the young leaders of diverse ethnicity who were part of the leadership team. I was amazed how they tutored everyone using technology that communicated with the older folks at the meeting. It didn't look like a typical church meeting. It was guided by visuals, graphs and expressions that young people understand. I asked the pastor why he had delegated such an

important meeting to the young people. His answer was simple: "The art of reverse mentoring." It was an opportunity for the older folks to be taught, mentored and equipped by the emerging leaders in an attempt to prepare for the future. According to the pastor: "They watch reality TV. They want to see and engage with real people and, as leaders, they want to learn from what real people go through."

Hypocritical leadership

Most leaders are a reflection of their background, exposure, education, culture and worldview. The culture of most BAME Christians does not allow a leader to exhibit weakness and vulnerability. This can mean leaders appear hypocritical with subtly compromised integrity. From the older generation's perspective, how can you appear weak and unsure to people who are looking up to a leader that shouldn't and must never have any failings? The younger generation have a different perspective. They are seeking leaders who are authentic and real, ready to admit failure, weakness and ignorance on some issues. From the older generation's viewpoint, this vulnerability is not an obvious qualification for leadership, but it is vital to engage the young adult from their position of weakness and then gradually journey with them to a place of maturity, while maintaining authentic engagement.

Communication

Social media and global digital communications have changed the world for young people. A new community of people has emerged, and the world has become a village that is so near and so real with no ethnic specifics.

Many of the younger generation don't have a particular leader that speaks into their lives; they have input from many sources across the globe across ethnic divides. For example, my 18-year-old daughter is British-born from Nigerian roots, but she connects with a church from Ghana in London and regularly connects with an online service from a majority-white church in America.

The playing field has changed if we really want to connect across different ethnicities. Modern communications have given the church different tools to express diversity and demonstrate inclusion of the younger generation.

Not having social media channels for the church is like shutting the church's front door to the colour-blind generation. Every leader must have a substantial communications team that understands the handles, the narratives and the images that will suit different platforms and mediums like Facebook, Twitter, Instagram, YouTube, webpages, podcasts etc.

Andy Frost

Andy Frost is director of Share Jesus International. His passion is to bring churches together to share in mission and community transformation. He is white British and presently works with Gather, developing church unity networks across the UK. He also helps to lead the London Mission Collective, collaborating on a variety of city-wide projects that help to unite London's diverse church networks in bringing about gospel transformation.

Many said it couldn't be done. London is more like a country than a city with a bustling nine million residents living across 33 disparate boroughs. It is one of the most expensive cities on Earth with a thriving mainstream cultural and arts scene. And the church in London is as diverse as the population it represents, often divided on grounds of theology, culture and style.

And yet, the vision we felt God was leading us into was a massive cultural and arts festival, that took the church outside of the confines of its building and put the Christian festival of Pentecost back on the map.

Share Jesus is a relatively small charity and this vision was deemed impossible by many. It would need too many of London's churches to commit to delivering the vision. For myself, I knew the festival was possible, but one of my greatest fears as I took the vision forward, was that it would be a bland, white, middle-class festival, lacking the multicultural vibrancy that London is famous for. I didn't want 100 homogenous events. I wanted to see the body of Christ coming together to celebrate the church's birthday.

I quickly learnt that, as a white, male leader, it was crucial for the team leading the festival to represent the church of London in a way that I couldn't on my own. If I was able to recruit an ethnically diverse team, from a variety of London's churches, then maybe, we could create a festival that really did represent the fullness of church in London. With a very limited budget, the team needed to both represent, and help me understand, the cultures of the city. It was a case of being intentional in connecting with younger leaders that could capture the vision with me.

Very practically, I learnt early on that the term 'gap year' was very narrow in its appeal. For a certain demographic, they didn't want a 'year out'. They wanted to progress in their calling and career, so I had to match the opportunities of helping to lead the festival with their aspirations. Rather than calling them interns, they were given organisational titles and business cards that would give them a greater respect in meetings and help them in their career progression longer term.

Having a culturally diverse team of 18 to 25-year olds also made me rethink how I lead. Too often I assumed what people's capacities and skills were from one initial interview, but as I was working with young leaders from a range of ethnicities, I discovered it was dangerous to put people in a box. One of the administrators was a talented spoken-word artist; one of the copy editors happened also to be a web developer; one of the graphic designers was also a talented worship leader.

When we work with a diverse team of young adults, we need to assume less and keep creating space for dialogue and feedback. We need to value each unique viewpoint. During this period, I discovered so much from the perspectives that were made available within the team around me. When we invite younger leaders from a mix of cultural backgrounds to share in a vision, the vision is enriched, and we get a wider understanding of what God is doing.

Pentecost Festival ran from 2008 to 2012 in the heart of London. We pulled it off, not only once but for five years running. Attracting 30,000 Londoners and tourists, the programme was anything but homogeneous. There were spoken-word nights in swanky bars; Bollywood performances in theatres; prominent scientists talking faith in university lecture halls; and young people campaigning for justice on the streets. There were hip-hop performances in parks; multicultural worship events in large auditoriums; gospel choirs on the steps of town halls; and an Asian food festival pouring out of a church onto the streets. It was a picture of Pentecost.

We wanted to see an ethnically-diverse festival, so we needed to model it first. If we want to see an ethically-diverse but united church, then we need to model it first.

Shantelle Johnson

Shantelle Johnson is communications manager at London City Mission. She is black Caribbean. Having grown up in a traditional, black-majority pentecostal church, Shantelle is passionate about seeing more churches that truly reflect their local communities, regardless of age, ethnicity, culture or class. She's particularly interested in seeing churches commit to discipleship and mentoring youth and young adults, to help them become strong leaders in their churches and communities.

I go to a truly diverse church. There's a huge difference in age groups, class and culture. Once a year we have an international day where 50-60 ethnicities are reflected and celebrated, which is beautiful to see. The church has successfully created pockets and places for celebrating diversity. There's not a dominant culture in the church, even though the headship is Nigerian, and the majority of the congregation is of West African origin. The consequence of mono-cultural leadership could be an environment where a particular culture and ethnic background dominates, but not here. What this church does well is offer opportunities for people to make suggestions. There is freedom for people to have a voice. And this is a balance they have managed to strike really well, so that everyone feels heard and the church adapts and changes.

The church's diversity is reflected in our small group setting, which creates good opportunities to talk to, and develop meaningful relationships with, people from different backgrounds.

The foundation of this church has always been rooted in teaching biblical doctrine so the congregation can be grounded in their faith. Everything points to Jesus and the sacrifice He made for all people, despite ethnicity or culture, at the cross of Calvary. This should be the focal point for all churches.

I feel the younger generation want strong theology and discipleship, and don't necessarily look to the church to be the primary place for their unique culture to thrive. We want a church where our shared kingdom culture thrives.

This isn't to say that young adults don't have an

interest in understanding or celebrating their culture, history and ethnic background. That's far from the truth. I'm of Barbadian heritage and like many West Indian young adults I know, we yearn to understand more about our incredible history and culture. But we don't hold the church responsible for providing us with that insight. Additionally, we are of a different generation and haven't faced the challenges that our grandparents or great grandparents did when they came to the UK. We have also grown up in diverse places. So, our experiences, perspectives and worldviews are different.

When I was younger, I went to a church that was established by West Indian people, mainly Jamaicans, who came to the UK between 1948 and 1971. They're known as the Windrush Generation. Many of them weren't welcome in the indigenous churches, which is why they set up their own. It created a home away from home I suppose. This church shaped me. It contributed to the strong foundation I have in my faith today, and my belief that Jesus is ultimately Lord over my life. It's where I saw dedication to prayer, amazing worship, and a reverence for the Word of God. It's home. Still today there are many churches that are extremely mono-cultural and which don't reflect the diversity of their local areas.

In exalting a particular culture, a church risks ostracising anyone who isn't of that culture. If a guest, or even a member, feels that they don't belong as a result of their cultural background, something has gone wrong. London, where I live, is a diverse place. If a young adult from a Turkish background, for example, comes into a church would they feel welcome?

Key principles

1. Become an advocate

- Speak out and advance the cause for intergenerational leadership
- Give loads of feedback
- Be authentic and transparent
- Use the younger generation in key strategic positions

2. Become a bridge

- Build bridges through mentoring and discipleship
- Foster an environment where intergenerational discipleship and mentorship, that goes both ways, is a natural part of church life, not just an official programme that people have to sign up to
- Build an integration bridge that includes young adults from different ethnic backgrounds in your conversations about shaping the culture of the church. Give them a voice and trust them with responsibility

3. Find a cause that will embrace inclusion and integration

- A cause in local and global mission
- A cause in projects, initiatives and events
- A cause for advocacy and justice

Questions

For personal reflection or discussion in your team

1. What are you doing to address the needs and the concerns of the emerging generation?

2. How can you create forums that welcome open dialogue with younger leaders?

3. How are you involving and learning from younger leaders?

4. Are there assumptions you've made about other generations or ethnicities, which might be hindering your willingness to make space for them? How could you confront them?

5. Where are the pockets and places for celebrating diversity?

6. What are your impossible dreams that you would love to see God do in your context?

The Future

Where do we go from here?

"It is simply impossible, with any shred of Christian integrity, to go on proclaiming that Jesus by His cross has abolished the old divisions and created a new single humanity of love, while at the same time we are contradicting our message by tolerating racial or social or other barriers within our church fellowship." Rev John Stott (*The Message of Ephesians*, IVP 1991)

A personal story – Steve and Ann Clifford

In the 1970s, Mr & Mrs Chhaganlall arrived in the UK from Mauritius in order to take up work in the NHS. They gave birth to two children, a boy and a girl. The girl, Asha, by now a woman, met our son Jake, they fell in love and were married. Asha Chhaganlall became Asha Clifford, and with great joy and thankfulness was welcomed into the heart of the Clifford family, as indeed Jake was welcomed by the Chhaganlalls. Within a few years, Judah, our first grandchild was born amidst much celebration. Both his Mauritian and British family lines bring a rich heritage and history. But before anything else, he is loved, yes as part of the Clifford Chhaganlall family here in the UK, but more importantly, as part of a spiritual family, the people of God – who, regardless of ethnic or cultural backgrounds, recognise each other as brothers and sisters in Christ. Thank God this is the church. History makes clear, we haven't always got it right and there are still many lessons to learn, but there must never be any doubt that we are family.

So, what is the future church in which Judah will grow up? Will it be a church that carries the hallmark of love, where the new command Jesus gave us can be seen by all?

"A new command I give you: love one another. As I have loved you, so you must love one another. By this everyone will know that you are my disciples, if you love one another" (John 13:34–35).

Judah will almost certainly be part of a church in a society, which is at times hostile to the Christian faith; where attitudes and beliefs that the church holds dear are no longer socially orthodox or indeed acceptable. But in such a world, will this church model another way of living? A church in which "the other" is always welcomed and all backgrounds of culture, class and ethnicity are welcomed to be part of the family?

We began this book by exploring the great prayer of Jesus in John 17, and it seems appropriate that we should return to this as we draw towards a conclusion.

"My prayer is not for them alone. I pray also for those who will believe in me through their message, that all of them may be one, Father, just as you are in me and I am in you. May they also be in us so that the world may believe that you have sent me. I have given them the glory that you gave me, that they may be one as we are one – I in them and you in me – so that they may be brought to complete unity. Then the world will know that you sent me and have loved them even as you have loved me" (John 17:20–23).

Jesus, hours before He goes to the cross, is praying for us 2000 years on: "those who will believe in me". He is praying that "they may be brought to complete unity"; the theme we've explored over the pages of this book, which is already being outworked in many church communities around the country. But Jesus brings within the prayer, a missional imperative "to let the world know". What is the world to know? It's there again in the prayer, he wants the world to know that Jesus is sent of the Father and that they are loved by the Father. Isn't this what we would want every person who walks the streets of the United Kingdom to know? Jesus makes clear that our unity and our oneness is one way which this message is made clear. For the Clifford family, our prayer is not simply that Judah will find faith, and be sustained in his faith, but that millions of others will come to the knowledge of the one who is our saviour and Lord.

A conclusion from Yemi

I want you to imagine what seems like an impossible dream today, as the new reality of the future. Imagine the people of God in the UK as an orchestra. Each of us represents a section of instruments in the orchestra. A solo performance does not make an orchestra, it takes accompanying instruments to lift an entire sound to a melodious level of beauty that will stir the emotions of any assembled crowd.

Granted each of us can perform alone, but it takes the participation of everyone to truly make music. Each one of us represents a race and culture that has distinct and separate qualities of sound. The truth is we can all stand alone, but when we become an orchestra, together we will produce a melody that is skilfully scored and executed; a harmony that fills the room and the soul, producing a sound takes people's breath away.

We are God's orchestra. The church should never be about one person standing out above others. Instead the emphasis should be on each person playing their unique, God-given part, blending together with all the other parts to produce an unbelievably moving sound.

I invite you to imagine!

Imagine a future where we will not define ourselves or be defined by the world as being black majority, ethnic minority or a white church.

Imagine a future where the discrimination, racism and prejudice, that make minority ethnic groups get second rate treatment, is eliminated.

Imagine a future where diverse ethnic people are welcomed across different church families to exhibit the beauty of their distinctiveness in serving God.

Imagine a future where churches across villages, towns and cities reflect the diversity of the people groups within their community.

Imagine churches now referenced as "All

Welcome" or "All Nations" being the true description of their congregation.

Imagine a bubbling and Spirit-filled church with younger generations that cross ethnic divides and cultural backgrounds.

Imagine a missional church with multi-ethnic leaders and pastoral teams.

Imagine a church that embraces God's culture of respect, honour and hospitality.

Imagine a church with good governance that is used as a mirror for comparison by secular organisations.

Imagine leadership teams that prefer others by being considerate of the needs of other ethnic groups.

Imagine a diverse leadership team that is committed for the long haul to work for authentic integration.

If we are to make a difference, we must first embrace the vision and see the dream of integration as a reality. We must challenge ourselves by being intentional in moving away from where we are to where we want to be. We must also develop strategies that suit our context to execute and then finally make a step-change into the future.

The impossible dream can become reality because with God all things are possible.

Further Reading and Resources

Lessons from the Journey

Lucy Olofinjana

Lucy is a born-and-bred south east Londoner and is passionate about Christian unity. She was the unity programmes manager at the Evangelical Alliance as the One People Commission began. Before that, she studied Social Anthropology and Development at the School of Oriental and African Studies (SOAS). Lucy is married to Israel, a Nigerian from a pentecostal background, who pastors Woolwich Central Baptist Church. They are blessed with a son, Iyanu.

Lucy was part of the journey as we sought to help the Evangelical Alliance to take multi-ethnic integration seriously. She recorded the lessons we learned, capturing the essence of the journey that we were taking, and her work became the inspiration for this book. Lucy's unique perspective as a white English woman married to a black Nigerian pastor, and her own studies, make her a woman with exceptional perception on these issues.

The Evangelical Alliance is committed to making evangelical unity across all ethnic expressions a key priority. It has been a challenging journey at times, but it has also been a wonderfully enriching journey, as we've built strong friendships across the wider expressions of our church family in the UK. It is also an ongoing journey as we are aware that there's still so much more to be done to live out those words of the gospel: "We are all one in Christ Jesus". We are aware that there's a danger of making generalisations in a document such as this, but we want to be as practical and helpful as possible. So here is our summary of what we have learnt along the way.

Four key lessons we've learnt

1. Build relationships

Build genuine friendships, spending time getting to know each other and building trust, being enriched by the new friendships across the wider church family.

2. Be intentional

Take time to meet people from other ethnic backgrounds one-to-one over tea and coffee, pizzas and curries, intentionally making sure you are allowing people from a range of backgrounds to shape what you do and how you do it.

3. Have honest conversations

As you listen to things from different perspectives, be open to being challenged, and to confront your blind-spots. This will lead to a stronger and more genuine unity.

4. Celebrate our diversity

It can be easy to focus on our differences and let them divide us, but the vibrant ethnic diversity within the UK church is truly something amazing to celebrate.

A summary of the journey

Intentionality is key

- We need to make efforts to consider ethnic diversity and representation in all that we are doing.
- Building relationships and trust is very important, and takes time and effort.
- Listening is very important – not just coming to people with our plans and asking for their backing, but listening to and being shaped by their perspectives.

Integration is the aim

The aim is to see integration of ethnic diversity within all that we do, within all our programmes, teams, structures and communications. Include as many different voices as you can around the leadership table. For the Evangelical Alliance that means it is not just the One People Commission team that is intentional about ethnic diversity. For example:

- The Public Leadership Advisory Group includes several BAME leaders with expertise in that area.
- The Great Commission website tells stories of people from a range of backgrounds.

Whilst we recognise that not everyone in the UK is living in multi-cultural communities, we do have *a message for all Christians in the UK* – to be aware that we are all part of a UK-wide evangelical community, which is ethnically diverse, and that we want to embrace and give thanks for this diversity.

We *must not assume* that people from different ethnic minority backgrounds all think or act in the same way. There are of course a wide range of views, opinions, personalities and ways of doing church, both between different ethnicities, and among people of the same ethnic group.

We *mustn't homogenise*, and must make sure we're listening to a range of voices and perspectives:

- Seeking to have a range of people and voices represented from around the globe.
- Recognising the different experiences/perspectives of people who've come to Britain as first-generation migrants, having grown up abroad, compared to those who are second, third, fourth, and fifth generation. This links to the importance of listening to young adults too.
- It's also important to be intentional about connecting with and hearing from BAME women, as well as men.

Honouring leaders is very important in many BAME cultures:

- It's respectful to refer to leaders by their title, eg Pastor or Rev or Dr:
  - some who are ordained prefer the title 'Rev' rather than 'Pastor', which can be given to someone who is not ordained/a formal minister
  - others who are not pastoring a church, but ministering in other ways, also prefer to use the title 'Rev'.
- We try to use very respectful and honouring language in our communications with leaders.
- Honouring also links to hospitality and food, which is important in many BAME cultures. Providing a good meal/lunch is a sign of respect and hospitality which is appreciated.
- Having a smart appearance for functions and meetings with BAME leaders is also a mark of respect.

Prayer is very important in many BAME church communities, therefore we always give time for prayer on our meeting agendas.

Generosity is a hallmark of many BAME churches – for example with many African leaders, they would be open to being asked directly when there is a financial need for a ministry or project, and many will respond generously.

Differences in communication style are important to understand:

- for example a face-to-face meeting is likely to open doors with many BAME leaders, and help to build trust and a strong relationship.
- A phone call is likely to be more successful than an email in getting a response.
- Text messages can also be effective, if you know the person well.

Racism, including within the church, can at times be quite subtle, and therefore harder to recognise:

- *A subtle condescending attitude. For example:*
  - that BAME leaders are not really qualified to speak with authority (this can be seen in reactions to leaders when they do

speak, or in what BAME leaders are asked to speak on).
  - that BAME leaders are only able to speak for BAME communities
  - that we only need BAME leaders' involvement to promote the plans which we have already come up with. This implies "we know best and we don't need your input".
- *Generalising/homogenising:*
  - Suggesting that a BAME leader can speak for or represent their entire race.
  - Assuming that all BAME people and communities think or experience things in the same way, and that hearing from, consulting or involving one BAME person is enough to hear the 'ethnic' or 'non-white' perspective.
- *Dismissing the experiences and realities* which BAME people share with us. Often this reveals a deep-seated attitude of "they don't really know what they're talking about; we know better".
- *Institutional structures which exclude* BAME representation:
  - Are the people making up the panels/groups/committees, which make key decisions about funding/appointments/nominations/the giving of grants from a diverse range of backgrounds? If those making the decisions are not representative, it is likely there will be bias in how these appointments are made and funding allocated.
  - Deep-seated misunderstandings/interpretations of how others do things can lead to discrimination/unconscious bias against people/churches from a BAME background.
- When challenging racism, *telling stories* can be an effective way of getting across challenging points and communicating the realities.

Some practical points...

When strategising/planning programmes or initiatives

- Ask BAME leaders to be *involved in shaping/planning* our programmes or initiatives – not just waiting until we've planned everything, and then asking for their backing/support/promotion. This was a key point which Steve heard when he visited BAME leaders in his early days as general director, before the One People Commission was founded.
- Have a range of BAME leaders as part of any *consultation/advisory/theology groups*.

When planning events

- Aim to have at least one *speaker* from a BAME background. Just as we are intentional about not having only male speakers, we should also be intentional about ethnic diversity.
- Avoid asking BAME people *only to speak/write* on BAME/ethnicity/racial issues, just as

women shouldn't only be asked to speak about gender/motherhood.

Food and hospitality are very important in many BAME cultures:

- When BAME leaders/ churches are hosting a meeting, they might want to provide the catering themselves, and often provide a very generous spread. However we mustn't assume that they are providing the catering.
- Some people from a BAME background don't like cold food and would much prefer a hot meal to sandwiches.
- In some BAME cultures, *Christians don't drink alcohol*. It is important to have soft drinks available. If it's an event mainly for OPC networks, we wouldn't provide alcohol.

Honouring leaders is important in many BAME cultures:

- If a BAME leader is hosting an event, consider buying them/their team a gift to express appreciation.
- Asking senior BAME leaders to pay to come to a fundraising event would be seen as dishonouring.
- Having a smart appearance for functions/ meetings with BAME leaders is also a mark of respect.

Prayer is also important in many BAME cultures, which is worth considering when planning events.

Many BAME leaders are *very generous* with their resources and buildings, and many would be open to being asked whether they could host meetings or services for example.

Communication styles vary. With RSVPs for meetings, some leaders respond better to emails with a follow-up text or phone call. It's also worth sending out dates well in advance, to allow as much time as possible to follow up RSVPs.

Publications and communications

- Try to use *writers* from a range of ethnic backgrounds.
- *Tell stories* from people and churches from different backgrounds.
- Making sure the *photos/images* you use in publications and on social media model ethnic diversity.
- Have a diverse representation of contributors on *theology;* not just asking BAME people to speak into a narrow range of issues.

Terminology:

- Terms to avoid:
  - instead of 'race', we prefer to use the language of 'ethnicity', 'different ethnicities' or 'culture' – 'race' tends to homogenise, whereas 'ethnicity' reflects the different cultures which we come from. Also language of 'race' has connotations of superiority/ inferiority.
  - avoid using the term 'the migrant church' – this implies that people of BAME background are migrants (here temporarily) rather than being a full part of British culture and society.
  - avoid using the term 'ethnic' on its own to describe people/things of a BAME/ethnic

minority background. Remember that white British is also an ethnicity!
    - Note that the term ‘English’ can be read as ‘white English’ by many people, therefore shouldn’t be used to describe ‘adults in England’.
- In terms of what language to use to describe people of an ethnic minority background, in truth there is no ideal term. Here are some options:
    - ‘Ethnic minority’ or ‘minority ethnic’ – some people don’t like using these terms as they imply being a minority/inferior in some way.
    - ‘BME’ (Black and minority ethnic) or ‘BAME’ (Black, Asian and minority ethnic) – some people don’t like using these terms as they sound like impersonal ‘labels’
    - ‘Black British’, ‘Asian British’ etc

Things to avoid

Things to avoid in our language/tone:

- See above re terminology – avoid using the terms ‘the migrant church’ and ‘ethnic’ on its own.
- Avoid using language which assumes that ethnic unity is a difficult thing which is very hard to achieve.
    - While acknowledging the challenges, we want to start from the premise that we are all God’s children, and one body in Christ.
    - We also want to celebrate our diversity and the richness which that brings, rather than seeing diversity as a negative challenge to overcome.

Avoid ‘us’ and ‘them’ language

- BAME Christians and churches are very much part of the evangelical constituency – therefore it’s about us together, not “them over there” and “us over here”.
- There can be a danger in our language (even within this book) that we sound like we are saying the Evangelical Alliance is white, and we engage with BAME Christians – whereas the Evangelical Alliance is the Alliance of the Evangelical Church, which in itself is ethnically diverse.
    - In his *Future First* research publication in June 2017, Peter Brierley reports that 40% of evangelicals in England are BAME, and 60% white.
    - In terms of the UK as a whole, we work with the estimate that 20-25% of the evangelical church is from a BAME background – while recognising that England has a lot more ethnic diversity than the Celtic nations.

Further Reading and Resources

Leading a Multicultural Church, Malcolm Patten, SPCK 2016

Building Cultural Intelligence in the Church and Ministry, Osoba O Otaigbe, Author House UK 2016

The Windrush Legacy, Faith in Migration DVD

One Day or One Week Training in Multicultural Worship, All Nations College

We Need To Talk About Race, Ben Lindsay, SPCK 2019

Crossing the Divide (A call to embrace diversity), Owen Hylton, IVP 2009

Partnership in Mission (A black majority church perspective on mission and church unity), Israel Olofinjana, Instant Apostle 2015

Building a Healthy Multiethnic Church, Mark Deymaz, Jossey Bass 2007

Lord Make Us One: But Not All The Same! Joel Edwards, Hodder & Stoughton Religious 1999

Turning the Tables on Mission (Stories of Christians from the Global South in the UK) Israel Olofinjana, Joel Edwards and Ram Gidoomal, Instant Apostle 2013